The Scandal of the Incarnation

The Scandal
of the
Incarnation:

Irenaeus *Against the Heresies*

Selected and with an introduction by
Hans Urs von Balthasar

Translated by John Saward

4 p.51

IGNATIUS PRESS   SAN FRANCISCO

Title of the German original
Irenäus: *Gott im Fleisch und Blut*
Ausgewähit und Ubertragen von Hans Urs von Balthasar
© 1981, Johannes Verlag, Einsiedeln

Cover design by Roxanne Mei Lum
Cover art: *Christ Mocked by Soldiers*
Georges Roualt (1932)
Oil on canvas, $36^{1}/_{4} \times 28^{1}/_{2}''$ (92.1 × 72.4 cm.)
Collection, The Museum of Modern Art, New York
(Given anonymously)
Photograph © 1990 The Museum of Modern Art, New York

ISBN 0—89870—315—8
Library of Congress catalogue number 90—82992
Printed in the United States of America

CONTENTS

INTRODUCTION

I

'So-called gnosis' was an enormous temptation in the early Christian Church. By contrast, persecution, even the bloodiest, posed far less of a threat to the Church's continuing purity and further development. Gnosticism had its roots in late antiquity, drew on oriental and Jewish sources, and multiplied into innumerable esoteric doctrines and sects. Then, like a vampire, the parasite took hold of the youthful bloom and vigour of Christianity. What made it so insidious was the fact that the Gnostics very often did not want to leave the Church. Instead, they claimed to be offering a superior and more authentic exposition of Holy Scripture, though, of course, this was only for the 'superior souls' ('the spiritual', 'the pneumatic'); the common folk ('the psychic') were left to get on with their crude practices. It is not hard to see how this kind of compartmentalizing of the Church's members, indeed of mankind as a whole, inevitably encouraged not only an excited craving for higher initiation, but also an almost unbounded arrogance in those who had moved from mere 'faith' to real, enlightened 'knowledge'.

All manner of attractions for the religious sensation-seeker were on sale at this gaudy funfair. Always in the background was the fundamental dogma of Gnosticism — the belief that the lower, material sphere, the 'flesh', the world of the 'psychic', was contemptible, something to be vanquished, while the higher, spiritual world was all that was excellent, the only thing worth cultivating. Sometimes extreme licentiousness was permitted or recommended, for after all 'to the pure all things are pure'; at other times, the rule would be a body-hating asceticism. What mattered most was the 'knowledge' that ensured spiritual power: the timetable for all the soul's journeys in the hereafter, the

1

ground plan and genealogy of all the cosmic spheres, the key to the riddles of nature, the knowledge of all the powers holding sway between earth and heaven, and, last but not least, a true anatomy of the Godhead itself. In fear and trembling, the adept gazed into the abyss of eternity. He could see, emerging from the eternal silence of the 'void', from the 'groundless' abyss of the absolute, a teeming mass of powers, 'Aeons' and divine 'emanations'. Being male and female, these mated with each other, forming 'couples' ('syzygies'), in order to produce new beings belonging to the divine world. One of these, just one among many, was the 'redeemer' of the world, the Christ.

Tragic scenes are played out in this eerie twilight zone between the unfathomable 'groundlessness' of the divine, on the one hand, and the earthly world (which is still a thing of the future), on the other. The projecting of tragedy into the realm of the divine shows that the fantastic Gnostic systems, though very different from each other, are myths in the proper sense of the word. They are, therefore, all in unambiguous opposition to the Christian view of the world. For the Christian, God's creation, in its material and spiritual totality, is 'very good'. But, for Gnosticism, the world always comes into existence as the result of a tragic accident, a disaster, a fall. In the first book of his work Against the Heresies, *Irenaeus tries to outline the diversity of these Gnostic myths. It will suffice here to list a few of their main themes.*

For example, one of the 'gods', forgetting his origins, sets himself up as creator of the world (demiurgos). *By his own power, and against the will of the Forefather* (propator), *he produces the earthly world, the realm of iron fate, of harsh 'justice', of bodiliness, of blind instinct. But, by cunning, an emissary of the supreme god penetrates the sphere of this antidivine Demiurge and goes down to earth. There, through initiation into the mysteries of the upper world, he redeems the elect (and only the elect!).*

In a second tragic myth, one of the Aeons that make up the 'divine Pleroma', namely, the daughter of God, Sophia (Achamoth), strays from the Pleroma; the material world arises out of her fears and tears, her 'secretions'. The Christ, who once again is seen as coming down from the world of sublimity to penetrate the world of poverty, eventually redeems her together with the higher spiritual souls.

It was Marcion who taught the most dangerous form of this mythical struggle of the gods, the most dangerous because it is the one that seems closest to Christianity and least burdened by fantasy. What is more, he is keen on scriptural exegesis. Marcion identifies the evil Demiurge with Yahweh, the Old Testament God of justice. The redeemer who sets us free from his tyranny is Jesus the Christ. According to Marcion, the teaching of Jesus has unfortunately been mixed up by the evangelists with elements from the Old Testament, from which it must be set free. The principle of justice and the principle of love are in stark opposition, as are the religion of works and the religion of grace, the religion of legal exteriority and spiritual interiority. This is the first systematic form of theological anti-Semitism.

The same conflict, the same dualism, runs through all the other systems of Gnosticism. In the earthly world it is reflected in the stark opposition of body and spirit. The bodily is regarded as something antidivine, which the 'spiritual' person leaves behind and beneath him if he is to be redeemed and returned, through secret knowledge, to the supermundane regions of pure spirit from which he fell. The inferior, animal souls are incapable of such an existence. Catholics are occasionally conceded an intermediate existence between the two spheres, but at the end of the world, they do not reach the highest of the heavenly spheres, but only the cosmic 'centre'. From this very general description, we can see that Gnosticism is radically anti-Christian. Irenaeus, with great perspicacity, understood this, and showed it up for what it was. For him, Christianity is about the divine and spiritual Word becoming flesh and body. The redemption depends on the real Incarnation, the real suffering on the Cross, and the real resurrection of the flesh. All three of these are a scandal for Gnosticism. On their view, Mary is not really Mother of God, and Christ did not really suffer — no, the heavenly Christ made off before the man Jesus suffered, and there can be no question at all of

3

an actual resurrection of the flesh. Underlying this refusal of the flesh and its saving role in the Incarnation is a confusion between the human spirit (nous) *and the divine Holy Spirit* (Pneuma Hagion). *The former puts itself in the place of the latter and identifies itself with it. And so the main object of Irenaeus' anti-Gnostic polemic is the salvific character of the Incarnation of God's Son and Word. Similarly, writing against Marcion, he proves the indispensability of the 'fleshly' Old Testament for the 'spiritual' New Testament by showing the old covenant to be basically an 'adaptation' of the divine Word to live in fleshly man, or, expressing the same idea from the other side, as the adaptation of earthly man to be the bearer of the divine Word.* Caro cardo salutis, *the flesh is the hinge, the decisive criterion, of salvation: this well-known saying of Tertullian, upon whom Irenaeus had a lasting influence, can in fact be regarded as the very centre of Irenaeus' theology.*

II

The Word of God first clashed with Gnostic myth in the second century, and nowhere more dramatically than in the work of Irenaeus. Given the fantastic forms of the mythology of the time, it all seems exotically remote. In fact, when we look more closely, we can see that we are dealing with a confrontation which has never ended and is constantly assuming new forms. The confusion mentioned above between the spirit of man and the Spirit of God characterizes all of mankind's more ambitious religious and philosophical speculations and mysticisms. It constantly devalues the sensible world, visible organization, the flesh, matter: these are mere 'appearances', either a deception or something to be seen through and overcome. Concealed behind them lies the only truth, the spirit, which must be set free and brought out into the open. This is the central axiom of all the religions of the East — from their ancient beginnings to their present-day posterity in this allegedly 'post-Christian age'. We shall see how hard it was for the Fathers after Irenaeus to ward off Gnostic infiltration. In the Middle Ages, from the remote Calabrian monastery of Fiore,

4

the doctrine of Abbot Joachim was to exert an incalculable influence on later generations which has lasted to the present day. He thought that the age of the Incarnation of the Second Person of the Blessed Trinity (together with the organized structure of His Church) would eventually 'dissolve' into an age of Pure (Holy!) Spirit. This spirit — passing through the stages of the Renaissance, the Enlightenment (Lessing), Idealism, and Marxism — degenerated into the purely human spirit of atheism.[1] Of course, the Jewish Kabbala and Gematria of the Middle Ages and the Renaissance were also of predominantly Gnostic origin. Jakob Böhme, with his far-reaching influence on Romanticism and Idealism, reintroduced a tragic dualism into the Godhead. This was the inspiration of Schelling and Baader. But it is above all the fundamental tendency of Hegel's philosophy which can be called Gnostic. For Hegel, everything material remains phenomenal and only finds its truth in the spiritual. The religious 'dualism' which distinguishes between pious consciousness and the Absolute is a mere 'image' (Vorstellung), *which, even in the case of the so-called 'absolute religion' of Christianity, has to be rejected in favour of all-encompassing absolute 'knowledge'. Ultimately, for man, there can be no more mystery about the divine Spirit.*

The Gnostic impulse secretly or openly animates all those modern world-views which see 'body' and 'spirit', bios and ethos, nature and God, in antagonism or opposition. Apparently irreconcilable schools of thought come together in the spirit of Marcion. Biologistic resentment against the Jewish spirit of the Old Testament feeds on it; it is no accident that Harnack erected a memorial to the old heretic. One of ancient Gnosticism's favourite doctrines, vigorously satirized by Irenaeus, is the glorification of the 'eternal quest', the idea being that the supreme principle, the 'Groundless One', is unknowable. It is not difficult to see why this emotional attachment to seeking, which despises finding as bourgeois, should have revived in our own times. But the clearest proof of the continuing relevance of the second-century struggle against Gnosticism is the fashionable interest, within the Christian Churches, in Zen meditation. This is essentially anti-Incarnational. All sensible images, all words and concepts must be removed, so that there is nothing left but the unfathomable void in which a supposedly superobjective insight (gnosis) can flourish. However mutually contradictory these currents of thought may at first sight appear to be, they are united in their 'spirtualizing' flight from matter and the 'flesh'. Modern materialism seems to be an exception, and yet it too is opposed to the Christian principle of Incarnation. At least in practice, it regards matter as something to be dominated, and in man himself as the way to power. Myth and Christianity are opposed on every point. Myth seeks the ascent of man to spirit; the Word of God seeks descent into flesh and blood. Myth wants power; revelation reveals the true power of God in the most extreme powerlessness. Myth wants knowledge; the Word of God asks for constant faith and, only within that faith, a growing, reverent understanding. Myth is the lightning that flashes when contradictory things collide — absolute knowledge, eternal quest; the revelation of God's Word is gentle patience amidst the intractable tensions of life. Myth tears God and world apart by trying to force them into a magical unity; the revelation of God's Word unites God and world by sealing the distance between them in the very intimacy of their communion. That is why myth eventually breaks up into the two irreconcilable halves of 'being as God' and 'tragic existence', while God's Word delivers man from both, for God incarnate, by His suffering in the flesh, has set us free from our tragedy.

Myth is unmasked by the Word of God. It is the outcome of man's desperate arrogance, his refusal to submit to God, his determination to make his own way to Heaven. Irenaeus did not need to speculate. All he had to do was let the Word of God speak for itself and show its inner logic, the logic of Old and New Testaments in their perpetual unity. The biblical way to God has been opened up by God Himself — God's Word is the way. And so, for the person willing to follow it in patience, it can lead to the divine destination, to the vision of God the Creator and Redeemer. By contrast, the Gnostic's self-devised ascent is bound to end, like the flight of Icarus, in a crash both tragic and grotesque. The surge beyond faith into the abyss of God ends in a blinded fall into *inhumanity. The Godhead that seemed to hold the promise of plenitude* (pleroma), *reveals itself to be anonymity, a silent void, the empty abyss of man himself, the projection of his own deficiency onto the wall of the absolute.*

III

In their epistles, St Paul and St John had begun the struggle against Gnosticism, which in their time was in its early stages. Even so, it was already showing its pernicious tendencies: promoting its seductive secret knowledge in the Christian communities, confusing simple believers, and spreading the first dangerous 'pluralism' within the unity of the faith. A real showdown only became possible when all the various systems of Gnosticism had been constructed. This took place towards the end of the second century. Irenaeus, Bishop of Lyons, was originally from Asia Minor. In his childhood he had known old Polycarp, the disciple of St John. In about AD 180 he composed his 'Five Books on the Unmasking and Refutation of the Falsely Named Gnosis'. This, apart from the short 'Proof of the Apostolic Preaching' and a few fragments, is the only work of his to come down to us. The five books were not written at the same time, but at intervals, though a logical plan underlies them. After describing the erroneous doctrines (Book 1) and reducing them to absurdity (Book 2), Irenaeus begins a detailed, positive refutation on the basis of Sacred Scripture. The truth of the Scriptures proves the uniqueness of God, the Creator of the world, the Lord of the Old Testament as well as of the New. The Scriptures also prove the uniqueness of the Word of God, who spoke and acted in the old covenant and became man in Jesus Christ (Book 3). The pedagogical meaning of the Old Testament is considered in the light of its fulfilment in the New (Book 4). The resurrection of the flesh, prepared for by the Eucharist, presupposes that matter has been created by God and is good (Book 5). These statements are, of course, only very general indications. The progress of the argument is impeded by all kinds of digressions and repetitions.

Nevertheless, this work is sufficient to qualify its author as indisputably the greatest theologian of his century. That is how he was regarded by experts on the theological tradition such as Tertullian, Eusebius, Theodoret, and Epiphanius, who showered their praise on him. Gnosticism was rampant in Irenaeus' day, and is constantly reviving in all the non-Christian religions and philosophies. As we have seen, he exposed it as an essentially anti-Christian religious experiment which destroys the psychosomatic unity of man. He refuted this system not by his own speculation, but by simply contemplating Christian revelation in its unity, by seeing its form. He is theology's founding father and a paradigmatic figure in its history. Immediately after his death, the clear lines which he drew become blurred. Tertullian, who had written a powerful treatise 'On the Flesh of Christ', defected to the 'spiritual Church' of the Montanists, thereby subscribing to one of the fundamental principles of Gnosticism. Not long after, the great Alexandrians, Clement and Origen, attempted to annex to Christian theology as much as they could of the speculative property of Gnosticism, and behind that, of Middle Platonism. The Council of Nicaea drew once more a clear dividing line between the Christian doctrine of the Trinity and the schema adopted by Arius of emanations from the primordial One. This was a rule for the whole Church, but it did not stop the debate with Greek thought for long. The exchanges continued, in ever new forms, throughout the whole of the Patristic period, in the Byzantine tradition, in the western Middle Ages, right up to the Renaissance and the age of Baroque. If one takes, so to speak, a bird's-eye view of it, Irenaeus' place in this convoluted story seems even more remarkable. He draws the battle-lines clearly and cleanly.

In fact, the demarcation is the exact opposite of what we are used to seeing now. Today Christianity is regarded as an 'otherworldly' religion, whereas pagan atheism claims to be an affirmation of life in this world. In the second century, Gnosticism, the anti-Christian experiment, was seen to be a flight from the world and the body, a pale and arid spiritualism. It replaced the real world — violent, indeed sinful, yet redeemable by God, and

8

actually redeemed through the Incarnation of the Word — with an imaginary world, thus splitting the one nature of man in two. Christianity, by contrast, proved its plausibility not least because it wholeheartedly acknowledged the goodness of creation, and gladly and bravely affirmed man, man threatened by destiny, sin, and death, as well as God.

To Gnosticism's separation of soul and body, spirit and flesh, pneumatic and animal existence, Christianity opposed the Incarnation of God. The fact that God has become man, indeed flesh, proves that the redemption and resurrection of the entire earthly world is not just a possibility but a reality. Against the Gnostic separation of the old and new covenants, Irenaeus taught the unity of the testaments in Christ: they were different, because they were different stages in the one divine education of the human race. In contrast to Gnosticism's cold presumption, he proclaimed God's patience, visible in Christ and His Passion, given to us as redemptive grace in the form of faith, hope and love, by means of which we preserve a patient and humble distance from the eternal God whom we can never exhaustively comprehend. This attitude is the fundamental condition of all redemption; indeed, it is redemption itself. Time after time, Irenaeus refers all the specific questions back to the simple issue of the sovereign God and the humbly submissive creature, the eternal majesty of Being in its Trinitarian vitality and the eternal poverty and yearning of Becoming in its brokenness and open-endedness.

For the Christian, this issue loses all shadow of tragedy. In Christ — and so from the side of God, not from the side of man — the gulf has been bridged. Man becomes the vessel of God, earth His dwelling-place. Bread and wine, the fruits of the earth, in their Eucharistic transformation, seal the redemption of the world and the gratitude of the creature. Everything in Irenaeus is bathed in a warm and radiant joy, a wise and majestic gentleness. True, his words of struggle are hard as iron and crystal clear. A compromise, a 'synthesis' of the Word of God and myth, never emerges, not even as a speculative possibility. But his struggle is not dialectical. He refutes by unmasking, or rather by showing the face of truth. He does not try to persuade by means of syllogisms; he lets the truth shine and warm like the sun. He has the patience of maturity; in fact, those two words — 'patience' and 'maturity' — constantly recur in decisive places. In the noblest sense of the word, he is naïve, as naïve as God's Word was in human form. In this sign He 'overcame the world'.

In what follows, we hope to provide a systematically arranged selection of texts from all that is extant of the works of Irenaeus, Bishop of Lyons. All selections are arbitrary. The long descriptions of the Gnostic systems, which contain little of interest to the modern reader, have been deliberately left aside. The same goes for the more detailed refutations of Gnostic doctrines. The short summary at the beginning of this introduction should be enough to enable the reader of the texts to understand the allusions to the theorems of Gnosticism and to put them into context. Of course, these texts do not give us a fully detailed and comprehensive picture of Irenaeus' teaching on many subjects — for example, the Trinity, the Incarnation of the Logos, the Church, Scripture and Tradition, and so on. However, it must be admitted that very often he does not go beyond hints and allusions, and so anyone who reads these texts carefully — and that is necessary! — will get a good idea of the essence of his theology. For him, the meaning of Scripture, as read in the Church and understood by her, is self-evident to anyone with eyes open enough to see. Everything in the Bible is 'certain, true and real' (omnia firma et vera et substantiam habentia, V 35, 2), though it is also clear that it is not meant to be a textbook leading us into total knowledge. Instead, it leads us to faith in Christ and in prayer to God for the wisdom and insight to 'understand the sayings of the prophets' (D 57). But to see the self-evident meaning of Scripture, we have to read it in the Church, in other words, in her publicly confessed and authenticated tradition, the tradition that has come down from the apostles. The contrast between the secret tradition of the Gnostics (secret and therefore uncontrollable and arbitrary) and the public character of the Church — in the provable apostolic succession and the exposition of the faith given by the bishops and pres-

byters — is absolutely fundamental for Irenaeus. The two things — Scripture and Tradition — reflect each other. Together they make up the regula veritatis *(what Tertullian calls the* regula fidei*), the normative confession of faith; it is this, claims Irenaeus, which is the 'true gnosis'. The theology of this first great Christian thinker may not be worked out to the last technical detail, but its basic intuition, its vision of what distinguishes the Church from heresy and the sects, is so clear and penetrating that, taken as a whole, it cannot fail to enlighten the unbiased observer.*

Hans Urs von Balthasar

1 H. de Lubac, *La postérité spirituelle de Joachim de Fiore*, 2 vols, (Paris, 1979, 1981).

A note on the translation

St Irenaeus' *Against the Heresies* has been preserved in a Latin version. Of the original Greek, we have only fragments; sections of the work are also extant in Armenian and Syriac. In the *Sources Chrétiennes* series (Nos 100, 152, 153, 210, 211, 263, 264, 293, 294), Adelin Rousseau and his colleagues have given us a critical edition of the Latin text together with a reconstructed Greek text. For this English edition of *God in Flesh and Blood*, I have translated the extracts from *Against the Heresies* directly from the *Sources Chrétiennes* edition. The passages from the *Demonstration of the Apostolic Preaching* have been translated from L. M. Froidevaux's French translation of the Armenian text (*Sources Chrétiennes* No 62).

John Saward

The sign of the Son of Man

The thought of Irenaeus forms a great axis. Its first movement is steep and Godward. From the icy arrogance and worldly secrecies of Gnosticism, it flies straight to the saving heights of the ever greater God, whom no finite mind can grasp. The other movement is broad, slow, heavy, a line drawn across the face of the earth. In contrast to the Gnostics' empty spiritualism and proud contempt for the body, he stubbornly refuses to let man cut himself off from the life of this world and escape into a pseudo-heavenly half-existence. Iranaeus is the outspoken champion of the 'realism' of Christian theology. If there is to be real redemption, this earth and no other, this body and no other, must have the capacity to take God's grace into itself.

At the centre of this axis is the image of the Son of Man, who unites heaven and earth. He is the first touchstone of Christian truth. Only in Him is there resolution of the paradox which Gnosticism tried in vain to master: God by nature is invisible, yet man by nature desires the vision of God.

But this uniting of God and world takes place in the Passion of Christ, when He is stretched out between height and depth, breadth and length. The cross-beams are the world's true centre, and since it is in this sign that all creation is redeemed, they become the 'watermark' of any kind of existence in the world.

The flesh will see God through the Incarnation of God's Word
(1) And the Word 'used to speak to Moses face to face, as a man speaks to his friend' (Ex. 33:11). Moses longed for an unveiled sight of the One with whom he spoke, and so he was addressed as follows: 'Stand on the top of the rock, and I will cover you with my hand. When my splendour passes by, you will see me from behind, but my face will not be shown you, for no man shall see my face and live' (cf Ex. 33:20ff). This signifies two things: first, that it is impossible for man to see God, and secondly, that, through the

wisdom of God, in the last days, man will see God 'on the top of the rock', that is to say, in His coming as man. That is why, as the Gospel tells us, [the Lord] conversed with [Moses] face to face on the top of a mountain, in the presence also of Elijah. At the end He fulfilled the ancient promise.   IV 20, 9

(2) Not one of the heretics is of the opinion that the Word was made flesh. If you examine their creeds carefully, you will find that, in every one of them, the Word of God is presented as without flesh and incapable of suffering, as is 'the Christ who is above'. Some say that He revealed Himself as a transfigured man, but was not born or made flesh. Others deny that He took human form at all. They say that He descended, in the form of a dove, on the Jesus born of Mary . . . and after He had announced the 'unknown Father', He went up again into the 'divine Pleroma' . . . The Lord's disciple shows all these people to be false witnesses when he says: 'And the Word was made flesh, and dwelt among us' (John 1:14).[1]   III 11, 3

(3) All the solemn declarations of the heretics come down ultimately to this: blasphemy against the Creator, denial of salvation to God's handiwork, which is what the flesh is.
                                                                    IV praef.

(4) To them the Word says, referring to His gift of grace: 'You are gods, and all of you the sons of the Most High, but you like men shall die' (Ps. 81:6f). He is without doubt addressing here those who do not want to accept the gift of adoption, but instead despise that pure birth which is the Incarnation of the Word, defrauding man of ascent to God and showing ingratitude to the divine Word who for them became incarnate. For it was for this that the Word of God became man and the Son of God became the Son of Man, namely, that man, commingled with the Word of God and receiving adoption, might become the son of God.
                                                                    III 19, 1

14

The Passion as the presupposition of redemption and union with God

(5) If He was not born, neither did He die. And if He did not die, neither did He rise from the dead. And if He did not rise from the dead, He did not conquer death and abolish its reign. And if He did not conquer death, how are we to ascend to the light, we who from the beginning have been subject to death? Those who rob man of redemption do not believe that God will raise man from the dead.   D 39

(6) He appeared as man in the fulness of time, and, being God's Word, He summed up in Himself all things in heaven and on earth. He united man with God and brought about communion between God and man.   D 30f

(7) 'A child is born to us, and a son is given to us, and the government is upon His shoulder' (Is. 9:6) . . . The words 'the government is upon His shoulder' figuratively signify the Cross, to which His arms were nailed. The Cross was and is ignominy for Him — and for us, for His sake. And yet it is the Cross which He calls His government, the sign of His kingship.   D 56

The cosmic dimension of the Cross

(8) By His obedience unto death on the Cross, He wiped out the ancient disobedience wrought on the tree. He is Himself the Word of almighty God, who in His invisible form pervades us all and encompasses the breadth and length, the height and depth, of the whole world, for by God's Word all things are guided and ordered. Now God's Son was also crucified in them [the four dimensions], since He has imprinted the form of the Cross on the universe. In becoming visible, He had to reveal the participation of the universe in His Cross. He wanted to display, in visible form, His activity in the visible realm, namely, that it is He who makes bright the heights, that is, what is in heaven, and reaches down into the depths, to what is under the

earth, and spreads out the length from East to West, and, like a pilot, guides the breadth from North to South, and calls together all the dispersed, from all the corners of the earth, to the knowledge of the Father.   D 34

Only if Christ has suffered, can He impose suffering

(9) If [as the Gnostics say] Christ was not supposed to suffer but fled from Jesus [during the Passion], what right did He have to exhort His disciples to take up their cross and follow Him (cf Matt. 16:24f)? For, according to the Gnostics, He Himself did not take up the Cross and abandoned the plan of suffering. He was not talking about the 'knowledge of the Cross above', as some of them have the audacity to claim, but about the suffering which He was to endure, and which awaited His disciples in the future. He proved this when He said: 'Whoever would save his life will lose it, and whoever loses his life will find it' (cf Matt. 16:25) . . . The same argument applies against those who say that He suffered only in appearance. If He did not really suffer, no gratitude is due to Him, since there was no Passion. And when He tells us, in our real sufferings, to endure the blows and to turn the other cheek, it will look like deception if He Himself has not suffered this in reality first . . . In fact, we should be 'above the Master', were we to suffer and sustain what the Master Himself had not suffered and sustained beforehand.   III 18, 5—6

---

1 St Augustine, too, later attributed the cause of all erroneous doctrine to the denial of the Incarnation of Christ (*Sermo* 183; PL 38, 968f).

The True God and the False God

The Gnostic image of God was the first great temptation which Christian thought had to overcome. Pagan polytheism was relatively easy to deal with. But here was an enticing system claiming to incorporate Christianity into its 'synthesis'. Creation — the greatest intellectual scandal of all — was simply explained away by means of its doctrine of emanation. And its romantic mythology had a special magic. Human beings, longing for redemption, were entranced by this philosophical world of dreams and fairy tales.

Irenaeus sets against this the humble and apparently unadorned image of God given in revelation. With the keenest perception, he sees the real motives behind the opposing system. I shall not here penetrate the tangle of the different Gnostic systems, but content myself with highlighting the main themes of the refutation. The hallmarks of Irenaeus' doctrine of God are an unrelenting emphasis on God's freedom with regard to the world and a deep reverence for the unfathomable mystery of His being.

We have no other access to the Trinity of God than salvation history, and every theology is well advised to avoid separating, even for a moment, its statements about the world-transcending 'immanent' Trinity from the 'economic' Trinity revealed in salvation history. All the Fathers before Nicaea vigorously adhered to this fundamental principle, but they often took it too far: they made the Godhead's inner Trinitarian life seem dependent on its planning of creation. Then the Logos appears as a 'means', a kind of divine pre-planning for creation. Irenaeus does not make this mistake. His thought moves with perfect precision from the economic to the immanent Trinity. The Son is said explicitly to be 'God', and, to get as far away as possible from the prying speculations of the Gnostics, Irenaeus plunges His eternal generation into such deep mystery that there is no chance at all of it appearing (as it does in, say, Justin or Tertullian) as the first stage of the creation of the cosmos. He is God's Word, the Self-Expression of the Father.

The Holy Spirit, too, identified with the 'Wisdom' of God, appears as the constant companion of the Father and the Son, preceding all creatures.

In contrast to the Gnostic 'emanations', which function as intermediaries between God and the world, Irenaeus, like the other early Fathers, asserts a clear concept of creation. Like St Paul and St John, he sees the creation taking place in the Logos, and the plan of creation is directed towards the summing up, in the fulness of time, of all things in the Son made man. That is why Irenaeus, without any subordination of them to the Father, describes the Son and the Spirit in terms of their function of making visible the invisible Father and indwelling creatures (he calls them the 'hands of the Father' at creation). Consider, for example, Irenaeus' assertion that the Father is essentially invisible, and that the Son makes Him visible. The first proposition is just a Scriptural truth, while the second obviously refers to the Son as revealed in salvation history and finally made man (cf III 11, 6, and the Sources Chrétiennes commentary volume for Book III, p. 282f).

Instead of boldly speculating about the processions in God, Irenaeus remains in reverence before the impenetrable mystery of the Godhead and removes the intra-divine high above all confusion with the world. In their speculations about the Logos, later Catholic theologians will try to illuminate the relationship between Father and Son by using the analogy of the relationship of the human word and thought to the mind. Irenaeus, for his part, prefers to emphasize the greater unlikeness in the likeness of this analogy.

A one-sided 'movement of descent' (from Father to Son to Spirit) is counterbalanced by the view that the Spirit is not only the One who leads to the Son, as the Son leads the Father, but also the Father's highest chosen gift to believers, in whom alone we can see the Son. The Holy Spirit is, therefore, all that is innermost, all that is most intimate, in God.

The God of Revelation

The Excellence of God

(10) The Father of all is far removed from the affections and passions proper to human beings. He is simple, non-composite, not made up of different members, altogether like and equal to Himself, because He is wholly intellect, wholly spirit, wholly mind, wholly thought, wholly reason, wholly hearing, wholly seeing, wholly light, and the whole source of all that is good. That is how men of religion and piety speak of God. But He is above all these properties too and therefore indescribable. He is rightly called the all-comprehending intellect, but He is not like the intellect of men. He is most aptly called 'light', but He is nothing like the light we know.   II 13, 3

The Trinity in itself and in creation and revelation

(11) Creatures must have the origin of their existence from some great cause. Now the origin of all things is God. He was not created by anyone, but everything was created by Him. The first thing to believe, therefore, is that there is one God, the Father, who created and ordered all things, calling into existence what did not exist. He contains all things, yet cannot Himself be contained. Now 'all things' includes this world of ours, with man in it. So this world of ours too was created by God.

So, then, there is one God, the Father, uncreated, invisible, creator of all things. There is no other God above Him and no other God beneath Him. God is rational, and therefore produced creatures by His Reason—Word. God is also spirit, and so He ordered all things through the Spirit, as the prophet says: 'By the word of the Lord the heavens were established, and all the power of them by His Spirit' (Ps. 32:6).

The Word 'establishes', that is, produces bodies and bestows permanence on what has come into existence, while the Spirit disposes and shapes the various 'powers'. The Word is, therefore, rightly called the Son, and the Spirit God's Wisdom. His apostle Paul puts it well: 'One God and Father of all, who is above all and with all and in all' (cf Eph. 4:6). The Father is 'above all', but the Word is 'with all', since it is through Him that everything was made by the Father. And 'in us all' is the Spirit, who cries 'Abba, Father' (cf Gal. 4:6), and forms man into the likeness of God. The Spirit manifests the Word, and so the prophets proclaimed the Son of God. But the Word lets the Spirit blow, and so it is He who speaks in the prophets and leads men back to the Father . . .

Our baptismal rebirth is accomplished through these articles: the Father grants us rebirth through His Son in the Holy Spirit. For those who have received the Spirit and bear Him within are led to the Word, that is to say, to the Son; and the Son presents them to the Father, and the Father makes them partakers of incorruptibility. Thus without the Spirit there is no seeing of the Word of God, and without the Son no one can approach the Father. For the Son is knowledge of the Father, and knowledge of the Son is through the Holy Spirit. But the Son, according to the Father's good pleasure, administers the Spirit, as the Father wills, to those to whom He wills.

The Father is called, in the Spirit, 'Most High' and 'Almighty' and 'Lord of Hosts', from which we learn what God truly is: creator of heaven and earth and all worlds, the maker of angels and of men, the Lord of all, the origin and giver of all things, merciful, compassionate, full of tenderness, good, just, the God of all, of the Jews as well as of the Gentiles . . . This God is glorified by His Word, who is His eternal Son, and by the Holy Spirit, who is the Wisdom of the Father of all. And their powers, the powers of the Word and of Wisdom, who are called Cherubim and Seraphim, also glorify God in songs of unceasing praise, and every creature in heaven gives glory to God, the Father of all.

D 4–5, 7, 10

(12) Thus the Father is Lord, and the Son is Lord, and the Father is God, and the Son is God, for He who is begotten of God is God. And in this way God is shown in His being and in the power of His nature to be one God, but in the administration and accomplishment of our redemption, He is Father and Son. For the Father is invisible and inaccessible to all creatures, and so it needed the Son to lead those who are to reach God into submission to the Father. David, too, speaks clearly and splendidly of Father and Son: 'Your throne, O God, is for ever and ever; you have loved justice, and hated iniquity, therefore God has anointed you with the oil of gladness above your fellows' (cf Ps. 44:7f). What this means is that the Son, being God, receives the throne of the everlasting kingdom from the Father, and the oil of anointing above His fellows. The oil of anointing is the Spirit, with whom He is anointed. And His 'fellows' are the prophets, the just, the apostles, and all who share in His Kingdom, in other words, His disciples.

D 47

The Trinitarian Christ
(13) The name 'Christ' implies the Anointer, the Anointed, and the Unction with which He is anointed. Now the Father is the Anointer, the Son is the Anointed, and the Spirit in whom He is anointed is the Unction.   III 18, 3

The Son and the Spirit serve the Father
(14) He is assisted in everything by His Offspring and Figuration, that is to say, the Son and the Spirit, the Word and Wisdom, whom all the angels serve, and to whom they are subject.   IV 7, 4

(15) It was through His tireless Word that [the Father] made all that He created.   II 2, 4

(16) [The Gnostics] say that the Word was emitted by the Intellect. Now we all know this is true of men. But God, who is above all things, is all Intellect and all Word; in Him there is nothing earlier and nothing later; He is wholly equal and identical and one. In such a God there can be no emission of the kind we have described. There is no error in saying that He is all vision and all hearing (in seeing, He hears, and in hearing, He sees), and so it can also be said that He is all 'Intellect' and all 'Word', that, in being Intellect, He is also Word, that the Word is this Intellect of His. This way of thinking about the Father of all is still inadequate, but it is more becoming than the attempt to apply to God's eternal Word the generation of the spoken human word, which implies that the former, like the latter, has a beginning and is involved in becoming. But how, then, does the Word of God, or rather, how does God Himself, since the Word is God, differ from the word of men if He follows the same order and mode of generation?[1] II 13, 8

The whole Godhead is common to the Divine Persons

(17) God is all Intellect and all Word, and so what He 'thinks', He also speaks, and what He 'speaks', He also thinks. For His thinking is His Word, and the Word is Mind, and the all-comprehending Mind is the Father.   II 28, 5

(18) It is false to say, as these men teach,[2] that the Word holds the third rank in generation and is ignorant of the Father. This may very likely be true of human generation, in the sense that people often do not know their parents, but it is absolutely impossible in the case of the Father's Word. For if He exists in the Father, He knows the One in whom He exists; in other words, He is not ignorant of Himself.   II 17, 8

The world is not the work of intermediaries

(19) This would imply that the angels were more powerful than God, or that He was negligent or inferior, or that He could not care less what happened in His own domain . . . If one would not dream of ascribing such conduct to a scrupulous man, how much less to God!   II 2, 1

(20) If it did not happen against His will,[3] but with His will and knowledge, as some of these men think, then the cause of creation will not be the angels or the Demiurge but the will of God. If He Himself made the Demiurge or the angels, or even if He was just the cause of their creation, He is to be seen as the maker of the world, because it was He who prepared the causes by which it was made. They maintain that the angels were produced by a long succession of intermediaries, or, according to Basilides, in the case of the Demiurge, by the 'primal Father'. Nevertheless, the cause of the things created must be attributed to the originator of the whole succession, just as the winning of a war is attributed to the king who prepared the causes of victory, or the founding of a city, indeed the carrying out of any project, is referred to the person who prepared the causes of success. We do not say that the axe cut the wood, nor that the saw divided it, but that the man . . . who produced the axe and the saw for that purpose did it. II 2, 3

(21) This idea [that subordinate beings were responsible for the material world] may well entice and seduce those who know nothing of God and imagine Him to be like needy human beings; they, after all, are incapable of making anything immediately and without assistance, but need all manner of instruments to produce what they want. It seems absolutely improbable to those who know that God, who needs nothing, created all things through His Word.   II 2, 4

The creation is not a 'fall'
into the void

In the beginning the world was perfect and created for perfection
(22) If things cannot be made better at the beginning,[4] how is improvement possible later on? Then again, how can they say that men are called to perfection, when the causes which allegedly made them (the Demiurge himself or the angels) are themselves said to be defective beings? And if, as they maintain, God in His goodness did at last take pity on men and bestowed perfection on them, He should surely first have pitied those who were the makers of man, and conferred perfection on *them!*   II 4, 2

In God there can be no 'void'
(23) Where does this 'void' come from?[5] Was it produced by the One they call the Father and Producer of all things? Is it equal in honour with the other Aeons, a kinsman of theirs? Is it perhaps even more ancient than they are? Now if it comes from the same Producer, it must be similar to the Producer and to the Producer's other products. And this makes it absolutely necessary that their 'Groundless One' (Bythus), along with 'Silence' (Sige), is similar to a void; in fact, it means he *is* a void. As for the other Aeons, they are the brothers of the void and so devoid of substance.

If, on the other hand, the void was not produced, it must have been born and generated from itself. But then it will be equal in time with the 'Groundless One', who, according to them, is the Father of All. Thus the void will be of the same nature and honour as the One they call the Father of All.
                    II 4, 1

In God's fulness it is impossible for anyone to create against His will
(24) Faced with these questions, they may well feel driven to despair. They may then confess that the Father of All contains all things, and that outside the Pleroma there is

nothing (because, if there were, it would necessarily be bounded and circumscribed by something greater than itself). They may also argue that, when they speak of 'without' and 'within', they are referring to knowledge and ignorance, not spatial distance . . . But then the question arises: what is this 'Groundless One'? What sort of being would tolerate a stain within His own bosom, and permit someone else to create or produce within His own domain and against His will? . . . They maintain that the light of this Father of theirs can fill and illuminate all that is within Him. If that is so, how can there be a 'void' or 'shadow' within the 'Pleroma' and 'Light of the Father'? They ought to be able to show us some unlighted and unoccupied place within the primal Father, or within the Pleroma, where the angels and the Demiurge were able to do what they wanted to do. And such a place cannot be just a hole in the corner, if it is to be the site on which creation in all its power and glory took place! . . . It would be a disgrace for the 'Light of the Father' to be incapable of illuminating and filling what is within Him. So when they claim that the world is a 'mistake', the result of a 'blunder', they are introducing mistakes and blunders into the Pleroma, into the bosom of the Father.

II 4, 2–3

Intermediaries are an insult to God

(25) It is impossible to think of someone's 'thought' or 'silence' having a separate existence, produced outside himself with a form of its own.   II 12, 2

(26) There cannot be 'word' where there is 'silence' [in the Gnostic sense], nor can there be 'silence' where there is 'word'.[6]   II 12, 5

(27) They apply to God things which happen to men, but then say that He is 'unknown' to all! For fear of belittling

Him, they deny that He created the world, but then endow Him with human affections and passions. If they knew the Scriptures and had been instructed by the truth, they would surely realize that God is not as men are, and 'His thoughts are not like the thoughts of men' (cf Is. 55:8).

II 13, 3

(28) You [Gnostics] are insufferable! You force the Word of God, the Creator, the Author and Maker of all things, into categories and numbers (sometimes thirty, sometimes twenty-four, at other times only six). You cut Him up into four syllables and thirty elements. You reduce the Lord of all, the One who founded the heavens, to the number eight hundred and eighty-eight. You treat Him like the alphabet. You subdivide the Father, who contains all but is contained by nothing, into a group of four, of eight, of ten, of twelve, hoping that these multiplications will help you to expound the nature of the Father, which, as you say yourself, is inexpressible and inconceivable.

I 15, 5

(29) I am well aware that, when you read through all this, dear friend, you will have a good laugh at such pretentious nonsense. But really we should feel sorry for people who, with their alphabet and their numbers, coldly and perversely mock a religion so noble, power so immense, so truly inexpressible, dispositions of God so striking.

I 16,3

God is not the image of the world
(30) Why is the division made into three rather than four, five, six, or some other number? [*Their answer is, of course, that the divine numbers are derived from the things in the world*] . . . But we are not asking them about the harmony of creation or human emotions, but about why this 'Pleroma', of which creation is said to be the image, is divided into groups of eight, ten, and twelve [*Perhaps they reply that the Father made the Pleroma as a 'schema' for the world*] . . . But this would mean that the Pleroma was not

made for its own sake, but for the sake of the world to be created as its image and in its likeness . . . but then the creature would be more honourable than the Pleroma![7]

II 15, 3

(31) The Aeons are supposed to be derived from the 'Word', the 'Word' from the 'Intellect', and the 'Intellect' from the 'Groundless One', just as lights are kindled from a light (for example, torches from a torch). If that is so, then presumably the Aeons differ from one another in generation and size. However, since they are of the same substance with the Author who produced them, then either they remain impassible, or their Father participates in passions. After all, a torch once kindled cannot later have a different kind of light from the one which preceded it. That is why their lights, when blended into one, return to the original unity; the single light then formed is the one which existed from the beginning. But it makes no sense to speak of some part of the light itself being 'younger' or 'older', because it is all one light.[8]   II 17, 4

Only the one True God can be the creator of the world

The Creator must be unlimited and omnipotent

(32) If man fails to grasp the fulness and greatness of His hand [in creation], how can anyone understand or know in his heart so great a God? Yet, as if they had measured and examined Him, scrutinized Him from every angle, they pretend that there is another pleroma of Aeons beyond Him, and another Father. Far from looking up to heavenly things, they truly descend into the profound abyss of madness. They say that their Father ends at the boundary of the Pleroma, while the Demiurge does not reach as far as the Pleroma. In other words, neither of them is perfect and all-encompassing. The Father lacks the whole of creation out-

27

side the Pleroma, and the Demiurge lacks the creation within the Pleroma. Neither of them can be the Lord of all.

It is clear to all that no one can fully show forth the grandeur of God from the things He has made. And anyone who thinks worthily of God will agree that His grandeur knows no defect, but contains all things, and extends even to us, and is with us. IV 19, 3

(33) Does their Father fail to bestow life when he could, or because he cannot? If he cannot, then this God allegedly superior to the Demiurge is neither omnipotent nor perfect. For the Demiurge clearly does bestow what this other being cannot. If, on the other hand, he could bestow life but just does not do it, then he is proved to be not a good Father but an envious and negligent one . . . If, therefore, by necessity or for some other reason, bodies capable of sharing in life are not vivified, their Father will be the slave of necessity and of that reason, no longer free and master of his own decisions.[9] V 4, 1—2

(34) It is unseemly to say of Him who is God over all that, though He is free and independent, He is a slave to necessity, that there are things which He has had to endure against His will. By speaking thus, they make necessity greater and more lordly than God. II 5, 4

The unity of God's planning and creation of the world
(35) If He knew in advance and contemplated in His mind the creation which was one day to arise in that place, then He is the One who created it; the One who created it is the One who formed it beforehand in Himself. So they should stop talking about the world being created by someone else. As soon as God's mind conceived it, the thing His mind conceived was made. For it was impossible for one being to conceive it in his mind and another to make the thing which the first one had in his mind conceived.

II 3, 1—2

28

(36) It is one and the same Lord who inflicts blindness on those who do not believe but set Him at naught (the sun, His creature, has much the same effect on those who, because of some infirmity of the eyes, cannot look upon its light), and bestows a fuller and greater illumination of the mind on those who believe and follow Him.   IV 29, 1

The unity of love and justice in God

(37) They claim that there is one God who judges and another who saves, thereby unwittingly robbing both deities of intelligence and justice. For if the judicial one is not also good, bestowing favours on the deserving and reproofs on those who ought to have them, then He will appear neither a just nor a wise judge. On the other hand, if the good God is only good and does not test the beneficiaries of His goodness, He will be outside of both justice and goodness; His goodness, if unaccompanied by judgement, will look like weakness, an inability to save all men. III 25, 2

1 This text is particularly remarkable, because, not long after Irenaeus, Tertullian and the Alexandrians took over the Gnostic idea of the spoken Word, thereby endangering the consubstantiality of the Son with the Father.

2 According to the Gnostics, the 'Abyss' (= the Father) first of all emitted 'Intellect', which in turn emitted the 'Word', who, because of His greater distance from Him, did not know the Father.

3 Even if the world had been created by angels — an hypothesis rejected in the texts that follow — it would only have been a case of God the Creator using them as secondary causes.

4 God could not create man in alienation from Himself. There must have been a primeval harmony between God and man.

5 The argument presupposes that the void, the nothing, is regarded as an absolute metaphysical principle, not just a way of expressing the creature's radical dependence on God, but a 'being' in its own right. Berdyaev was fond of this Gnostic doctrine.

6 In other words, instead of the mutual indwelling of the Divine Persons, Gnosticism posits a mutual limitation of principles, which destroys the idea of God.

7 In other words, for Gnosticism, as later for Feuerbach, Nietzsche, and Marx, man is the inventor of God.

8 That is why, after Nicaea, the Fathers applied the credal image of enkindling ('Light from Light') to the Trinity.

9 A significant statement: God cannot come *under* the category of 'reason for' (as He does for Descartes). Cf Jean-Luc Marion, *La théologie blanche de Descartes* (Paris, 1981).

Faith and Gnosis

If God is unbounded being, the world cannot be something that 'fell' from Him to be outside Him. And if He is the perfection of self-possessed freedom, the world cannot be a natural 'emanation' from His being. The Gnostics tried to explain the origin of the world, the origin of matter, in terms of a series of transitions between the Groundless One and us. Christianity replaced this with the idea of the creature's direct relationship, stark yet serene, with the eternal God. We cannot distance ourselves from Him, nor can the existence of creation be 'derived' from anywhere or be explained as necessary.

Now if the world is in God, it is impossible for Him to be absolutely hidden from it. Creatureliness, by its very boundaries and limitedness, reveals the existence of Him who is Creator and Lord. But this 'knowledge' of His existence demands of the creature the fundamental act of faith, that is to say, a humble, trusting, free submission to the Lord who eludes every attempt at capture.

Gnosticism refuses to make this fundamental act. It wants to get to know all of God's mysteries by its own powers. However surprising it may seem, it does appeal to the Scriptures, and so it is forced to posit a secret tradition, coming down from Jesus and the apostles, alongside the official proclamation of God for the simple. However, the attempt to take hold of God by force inevitably falls into the 'void' (the supreme God is, of course, mere 'silence' beyond the Word of revelation), and so the struggle of the 'eternal quest' is prized more highly than the bliss of discovery.

Irenaeus shows the secret wisdom of his opponents to be nothing but arrogance and folly, and convicts it of contradiction. This contradiction, which makes Gnosticism the forerunner of later 'dialectical' thought, is resolved in Christianity in the fundamental relationship of analogy between God and the world. Man, *composed of body and soul, is made in the 'image and likeness of God', who towers above him in (greater) unlikeness.*

The world is in God

(38) They must admit that the Father is a 'void', or that everything within Him equally partakes in the Father. It is like making circles, or round or square figures, in water; they will all equally partake of water. Or again, shapes formed in the air necessarily partake of air; those formed in light, of light. The same must be true of the Aeons within the Father; they must all partake of the Father, ignorance having no place among them. What else can be meant by partaking of the Father who fills all things? If He really fills all things, there can be no room for ignorance.

This demolishes their whole theory of the 'work of degeneracy', about the production of matter and the rest of the world's creation being due essentially to passion and ignorance. If, on the other hand, they admit that their Father is a void, they fall into the greatest blasphemy; they deny His spiritual nature. For how can He be a spiritual being, if He cannot fill even the things within Him?

II 13, 7

(39) We were created along with those things contained by Him. It is He of whom Scripture says, 'And God formed man, taking clay of the earth, and breathed into his face the breath of life' (cf Gen. 2:7). It was not angels, then, who made or formed us. Angels could not make an image of God, nor could some 'power' remotely distant from the Father of all, nor could anyone except the true God. Nor did God need any of these to carry out what He had decided beforehand within Himself should be done. As if He did not have His hands! For the Word and Wisdom, the Son

31

and the Spirit, were always with Him. Through Them and in Them He freely and spontaneously created all things.

IV 20, 1

(40) 'From the rising of the sun to the going down of the same, my name will be glorified among the Gentiles' (Mal. 1:10) . . . Now what other name is glorified among the Gentiles than that of Our Lord, by whom the Father is glorified, and man is glorified? He calls it His own name, because it is His own Son's name, and man was made by Him. If a king painted a picture of his son, he would be right to call it his own for two reasons: first, because it is a picture of his son, and secondly, because he himself painted it.

IV 17, 6

(41) How could either the angels or the 'Maker of the World' [of the Gnostics] have been ignorant of the supreme God, seeing that they were His property and His creatures, and were contained by Him? He may have been invisible to them because of His supereminence, but because of His providence, by no means could He have been unknown to them. By descent, they may have been, as the heretics say, very far from Him, but since His sovereignty extended over all, they ought to have known their Sovereign, and this above all they should have seen: that He who created them is Lord of all. For God, invisible by nature, is mighty, and confers on all a great mental intuition and perception of His most mighty, yes, almighty greatness. Therefore, though 'no one knows the Father except the Son, nor the Son except the Father, and those to whom the Son has revealed Him' (cf Matt. 11:27), yet all beings know this fact at least, because reason, implanted in their minds, moves them, and reveals to them that there is one God, the Lord of all.

Consequently, all things are subject to the name of Him who is the Most High and Almighty. By calling upon Him, even before the coming of Our Lord, men were saved from evil spirits, from all demons, and from every apostate power. I do not mean that these earthly spirits or demons had seen Him, but they did know of the existence of Him who is God over all, at whose invocation they trembled, as does all creation.   II 6, 1—2

(42) Creation shows its Creator, and what is made suggests its Maker.   II 9, 1

The knowledge of God as faith in God

(43) What is He like? How great is He? Since He who 'works all in all' (cf 1 Cor. 12:6) is God, He is invisible and inexpressible to all He has made, but by no means unknown. For all creatures learn from His Word that there is one God and Father, who contains all things in Himself and grants existence to all, as it says in the Gospel: 'No one has ever seen God; the only Son, who is in the bosom of the Father, he has made Him known' (John 1:18).

(44) To give the impression that they can explain the origin of matter, [the Gnostics] have collected a multitude of vain discourses, thereby proving their unbelief. They do not believe that, as He willed, God out of nothing created all things that they might exist (cf Wisd. 1:14), using as 'matter' only His will and power. They do not believe in what really exists, and have fallen into belief in what does not exist.   II 10, 2

(45) All those who hoped in Him believed in Him, all those, that is, who had foretold His coming and served His saving plans.   IV 27, 2

(46) To believe in Him is to do His will . . . Through the Word made visible and palpable, the Father was revealed. And though all did not in the same way believe, they nonetheless saw the Father in the Son . . . All see and speak of the Son and the Father, but not all believe.   IV 6, 5—6

(47) Not only in works, but also in faith, God has safeguarded the freedom and self-determination of man.

IV 37, 5

The arrogance of Gnosticism

Their ridiculous theory of creation

(48) They tell us that moist substance proceeded from the tears of Achamoth, lucid substance from her smile, solid substance from her sadness, mobile substance from her fear. Here, they say, puffing themselves up, is the highest wisdom. In fact, it deserves nothing but contempt; it is truly ridiculous. Ignorant of the power of a spiritual and divine substance, they do not believe that God, who is mighty and rich in all things, created matter. Instead, they believe that their 'Mother', whom they call 'woman from woman', produced the vast matter of creation out of the passions mentioned above! They ask where the Maker obtained the matter of creation. But they do not ask where their 'Mother' of theirs . . . obtained all those tears, all that sweat and sadness, and all the other material things she emitted!

But to ascribe the reality of created things to the power and will of the God of all is credible, acceptable, and coherent. It can rightly be said: 'What is impossible with men is possible with God' (Luke 18:27). Men cannot make anything out of nothing, but only out of already existing matter. God, however, is superior to men, because He calls

34

into being the matter of His creation when previously it did
not exist.   II 10, 3—4

The presumption of absolute knowledge

(49) [The Gnostic] regards himself as greater and of higher
authority than the prophetic spirit, though he is but a man.
                                                          I 13, 4

(50) They explain the birth of God's Word, of Him who is
Truth and Life, indeed Intellect; they act as midwife to the
emanations from the Godhead.   II 14, 8

(51) We who still live on earth do not yet sit beside God's
throne . . . As long as we are on earth, as St Paul says, 'we
know in part and prophesy in part' (cf 1 Cor. 13:9). If, then,
we only know in part, we ought to leave all difficult questions to Him who in part gives us His grace . . . In trying to
investigate things which are above us and at present
beyond our reach, we become so arrogant that we treat God
like a book to be opened and act as if we had already found
the unfindable. We talk stupidly about emanations and
claim that God, the Maker of all things, derived His substance from 'degeneration' and 'ignorance', thereby using a
godless argument against God.   II 28, 7

(52) Perfect redemption, they say, is knowledge of the
unspeakable majesty.   I 21, 4

(53) [Like the Jews] they claim to observe more than is
prescribed, as if they preferred their own zeal to God
Himself.   IV 11, 4

(54) But we are not more zealous than God, and we cannot
be above the Master.   IV 31, 1

(55) If they are superior to Him, their deeds should prove
it! . . . The words of Scripture, 'Seek and you will find'

(Matt. 7:7), were spoken, according to their interpretation, so that they should find themselves to be superior to the Maker of the world. They say that they are greater and better than God, calling themselves 'pneumatic', spiritual, and the Maker of the world 'psychic', animal. For this reason, they say, [at the end of time] they will rise above God and enter the Pleroma, while God remains in the intermediate place. So, then, let them prove by their works that they are superior to the Creator! . . .

However, the Maker of the world is the Spirit of God and not a 'psychic' being, otherwise He would never have created spiritual things. If He is 'psychic', let the heretics tell us who made spiritual things. They have no proof to show that this was done by the conception of their 'Mother', which is what they say they are. Far from being able to produce a spiritual entity, they cannot even create a fly or gnat or some other pitiful little creature independently of that natural process through which animals have been and are still produced by God, that is to say, by the deposition of seed in those that are of the same species. Nor did the 'Mother' make anything by herself, because they say that she produced the Maker of the world and Lord of the universe. They call Him who is Maker and Lord of the universe 'psychic', but themselves they call 'pneumatic', yet they are not makers of a single thing, nor lords of anything outside of themselves, not even of their own bodies! What is more, these people who call themselves 'spiritual' and 'superior to the Creator' often, against their will, suffer much bodily pain.   II 30, 2 and 8

The collapse of Gnosticism

Eternal quest

(56) 'Progress' is alleged to be finding another Father beyond the one proclaimed from the beginning, and then,

beyond the one supposed to have been discovered in second place, a third, and beyond the third a fourth, and then another, and then another . . . The person who thinks himself 'progressive' in this sense will never rest in one God. Driven from Him Who Is, he turns backwards, and sets off on an eternal 'quest' for God. But he will never find Him. He will just swim for ever in an abyss of 'incomprehensibility' — unless, converted and repentant, he returns to the place from which he was cast out, and confesses and believes in the one God, the Father, the Creator, announced by the law and the prophets and borne witness to by Christian.

IV 9, 3

(57) All heretics are like this. They imagine that they have found something higher than the truth . . . They set off on all kinds of uncertain paths, holding now one opinion, now another, on the same subject! They are like the blind who lead the blind and rightly fall into the ditch of ignorance at their feet. They are always seeking, but they never find the truth . . . Their thoughts soar above the permitted measure of thought. That is why the apostle says: 'Do not think more loftily than you ought to think, but think prudently' (cf Rom. 12:3). He is warning us not to taste the knowledge of the Gnostics, which 'thinks more loftily than it ought to think', and leads to our banishment from the 'paradise of life'.

V 20, 2

Evasive silence

(58) They have huge disagreements on a single point, conflicting opinions about the same Scriptures. When one and the same passage is read out, they all knit their brows and shake their heads and say that, of course, it is a very profound text, that not everyone can grasp the great thoughts it contains, and that silence is therefore the chief thing among the wise. In fact, their silence must be a replica of the 'Silence' above! And so they go their separate ways, ways as many as their numbers, spawning all these

opinions about the same subject, carrying their subtleties deep within themselves.

When they do eventually agree among themselves about what is foretold in the Scriptures, we shall still confute them. Meanwhile, with their wrong opinions, with their manifest failure to agree about the same set of words, they refute themselves. We, however, follow as our teacher the one and only true Lord and take His words as our rule of truth.
IV 35, 4

The 'God beyond God' is unrelated to anything

(59) Alienated from the truth, they are bound to wallow in total error, to be tossed to and fro by it. At different times they think different things about the same subject. They never have a settled opinion. They want to be verbal sophists rather than disciples of the truth. They are not built on a rock, but on sand, sand containing a multitude of stones.

And so they manufacture a multitude of gods. Their excuse is always that they are 'seekers'. In fact, they are blind, and they will never be able to find anything. For they blaspheme the Creator, Him who is truly God, who gives the power to find. They imagine that above God they have found another god, or another 'pleroma', or another 'economy'. Therefore, the light which comes from God does not enlighten them, because they have dishonoured and despised God. They regard Him as paltry, because in His love and immense kindness He has come within reach of human knowledge. Of course, this is not knowledge according to His greatness or substance, for that is something no one has ever measured or handled. No, I am talking about the the knowledge by which we know that He who made and formed us, who breathed into us the breath of life, who nourishes us by means of creation, establishing all things by His Word, ordering them in His Wisdom, that it is He who is the only true God. They, however, dream of a non-existent deity above Him, so that they will be regarded

38

as having discovered the 'great God', whom no one can know, who does not communicate with the human race, who does not direct the affairs of earth. In other words, they have discovered the god of Epicurus, who does nothing for himself or for anyone else, a god without providence.

III 24, 2

The Contradiction of Gnosticism

(60) [Sophia's][1] idea of seeking the perfect Father, her desire to penetrate and comprehend him, could not involve ignorance or passion — not in a spiritual Aeon! No, it meant rather perfection and impassibility. After all, they themselves are only human beings, and yet when they apply their minds to the One before them, when in some way they already comprehend Him and are established in their knowledge of Him, they do not say that they are in a passion of perplexity, but rather in the knowledge and apprehension of the truth. They claim that when the Saviour said the words 'Seek and you will find' to his disciples, he meant that they should search for the One whom the Gnostics' imagination has placed above the Creator of all things — the ineffable 'Groundless One'. They claim to be perfect themselves, because, even while still on earth, in seeking they have found the Perfect One. And yet they say that the totally spiritual Aeon who dwells within the Pleroma, by seeking the Forefather, by trying to penetrate his greatness, by yearning to know the truth of the Father, fell into passion, into such a passion, in fact, that, had the Power who upholds all things not intervened, she would have been dissolved into the universal substance and annihilated.

II 18, 6

(61) The Passion of Christ is not like the passion of the Aeon, nor did it take place in similar circumstances. The Aeon suffered a passion of dissolution and destruction, so much so that she who suffered was in danger of being cor-

rupted. But Christ our Lord suffered a strong and unflinching Passion. Not only was He Himself not in danger of being corrupted, He also strengthened corrupted man with His power and called him back to incorruption. The Aeon suffered her passion while seeking the Father, whom she was incapable of finding, whereas our Lord suffered in order to bring back to the knowledge and presence of the Father those who had strayed.   II 20, 3

(62) 'Seek and you will find.' The Lord makes His disciples perfect in their seeking *and* in their finding of the Father. By contrast, the 'superior Christ' [of the Gnostics] makes them perfect by ordering the Aeons not to seek the Father on the grounds that, however hard they try, they will not find Him. So the Gnostics call themselves perfect for having found their 'Groundless One', while the Aeons are perfect because they have been persuaded that the One they seek is unsearchable!   II 18, 3

Humility and the knowledge of God

(63) At this point someone may raise the objection: 'Is it without reason and by chance that the imposition of names, the election of the apostles, the activity of the Lord, and the arrangement of created things are what they are?' To this we say, 'Certainly not! It is with great wisdom and delicate care that God confers proportion and harmony on what He has made, both the things of old and all that His Word has accomplished in the latest times.' People should not link all these with the number thirty,[2] but rather with the meaning or reason which underlies them. We cannot investigate God by means of numbers and syllables and letters; they are too many and various to make that a reliable way of proceeding. Someone may construct a valid

theory out of numbers, but these same evidences can then be applied abusively against the truth; they can be turned in many different directions. No, what we have to do is correlate the numbers themselves, and the things which have been made, with the solid truth which underlies them. It is not the rule which comes from the numbers, but the numbers which come from the rule. God does not come from creatures; no, creatures come from God. Everything comes from one and the same God.

Created things, in their great number and diversity, fit beautifully and harmoniously into the creation as a whole. And yet, when viewed individually, they appear discordant and opposed to each other, just as the sound of the lute makes a single harmonious melody out of many and opposite notes by means of the intervals between them. The lover of truth must not be deceived, therefore, by the interval between the different notes, nor imagine that this note was the work of one artist and author, and that note due to another, nor think that one person fitted the treble, another the bass, and yet another the tenor strings. He must not forget that one and the same Artist was responsible for the wisdom, justice, goodness, and munificence of the whole work. And those who listen to the melody ought to praise and glorify the Artist, and admire the tension of some notes, appreciate the relaxation in others, enjoy the moderation of those between the two extremes. Recalling that some things are symbols, they will consider what it is that each thing points to and what causes it. But they will never alter the rule, nor stray from the Artist, nor abandon faith in the one God who made all things, nor blaspheme our Creator.

When someone fails to find the cause of all that he is investigating, he should recall that man is infinitely inferior to God . . . Man, you are not uncreated, and you have not existed from eternity with God, as His own Word has done. No, by His overflowing goodness you received the beginning of your existence, and have gradually learned from the Word the dispositions of the God who made you.

So keep your knowledge in its proper place. In ignorance of the good, do not try to rise above God Himself, for He cannot be surpassed. Do not look for anything above the Creator, for you will not find it; your Maker is without limits. And do not dream up some other Father above God, as if you had taken all His measurements, as if you had explored His entire creation, as if you had considered His whole depth and length and height. Your dreaming will come to nothing. Thinking against nature, you will become foolish. And if you persist, you will fall into insanity, regarding yourself as loftier and better than your own Creator, imagining that you can pass through and beyond the realms of God. II 25, 2—4

God's incomprehensible grandeur known because of His love

(64) God is above all [earthly names], and therefore inexpressible. He can well and rightly be called an all-comprehending intellect, but He is not like the intellect of men. He is most accurately described as light, but He is nothing like the light that we know. In fact, in every respect, the Father of all is unlike the littleness of men. Although, because of His love, we can use these words to speak of Him, we know, because of His greatness, that He is above them. II 13, 4

(65) As regards His grandeur, we cannot know God, for it is impossible to measure the Father. But as regards His love (for that is what leads us through the Word to God), those who obey Him are evermore learning that there is such a great God. IV 20, 1

(66) As regards His grandeur, He is unknown to all who have been made by Him, for no one has ever scaled the heights of God, neither the ancients nor the men of today.

But as regards His love, He is evermore known through the One through whom He made all things. This is His Word, our Lord Jesus Christ, who in the last times became man among men, in order to join the end to the beginning, that is, man to God. That is why the prophets, receiving the prophetic charism from the same Word, foretold His coming in the flesh, which, by the Father's good pleasure, has accomplished the blending and communion of God and man. From the beginning, the Word of God foretold that God would be seen by men and hold converse with them upon earth (cf Baruch 3:38). He would speak with them and be present to His own creation, thus saving it. He would become perceptible by it, thus 'freeing us from the hands of all who hate us'(Luke 1:71), that is to say, from every spirit of wickedness, and causing us to 'serve Him in holiness and justice all the days of our life' (ibid., vv. 74—75), in order that man, having embraced the Spirit of God, might pass into the Father's glory.   IV 20, 4

(67) As regards His grandeur and indescribable glory, 'no one shall see God and live' (cf Ex. 33:20), for the Father is incomprehensible. But as regards His love and kindness towards men, and because He can do all things, He grants to those who love Him the privilege of seeing Him. The prophets foretold this, for 'what is impossible to men is possible to God' (Luke 18:27). Man by his own powers cannot see God, but if He so wills it, God can be seen by men: by whom He wills and when He wills and as He wills.
                    IV 20, 5

Love is the way to God
(68) St Paul says that . . . without love for God, there is no value in knowledge, nor in the understanding of mysteries, nor in faith, nor in prophecy. They are all hollow and vain without love. He says that it is love which makes man perfect, and that he who loves God is perfect in this world and

in the world to come. We shall never cease to love God, but the more we behold Him, the more we shall love Him.

IV 12, 2

(69) Love is the most excellent gift, more precious than knowledge, more glorious than prophecy, superior to all the other charisms.

IV 33, 8

Ultimately, God can be known only through God

(70) 'No one has ever seen God. The only-begotten Son, who is in the bosom of the Father, He has made Him known' (John 1:18). From the beginning, the Son is the revealer of the Father, since from the beginning He is with the Father. At the fitting time, and for our profit, He has shown the human race, in a rational and harmonious way, the prophetic visions, the diversity of graces, His own ministrations, and the glorification of the Father. For where there is rationality, there is harmony, and where there is harmony, there is a fitting time, and where there is a fitting time, there is profit. That is why the Word became the dispenser of His Father's grace for the profit of men. It was for them that He accomplished such great dispositions, showing God to men, presenting man to God. He safeguarded the invisibility of the Father, lest man become the despiser of God, and so that he might always have something towards which he could advance. At the same time He made God visible to men through many dispensations, lest man, wholly bereft of God, should cease to exist. For the glory of God is the living man, and the life of man is the vision of God.

IV 20, 6–7

(71) How can God be unknown if He is known by [the Gnostics]? Whatever is known, even by just a few, is not

unknown. The Lord did not say that the Father and the Son could not be known at all, for in that case His coming would have been pointless. ['No one knows the Son except the Father, and no one knows the Father except the Son and anyone to whom the Son chooses to reveal Him' (Matt. 11:27)]. Why did He come here? To tell us: 'Do not seek God, because He is unknowable, and you will never find Him'? That is what Christ is supposed to have said, according to the lies of the Valentinians, to these Aeons of theirs. It is utter nonsense! What the Lord really taught is this: no one can know God unless God teaches him; in other words, without God, God cannot be known. What is more, it is the Father's will that God be known.   IV 6, 4

(72) No one can know the Father without the Word of God, that is to say, unless the Son reveals Him, nor can one know the Son without the good pleasure of the Father (cf Matt. 11:26f).   IV 6, 3

(73) The Son leads men to the Father, but the Father reveals to them the Son.   III 13, 2

From Old Covenant to New
(74) This is why the Jews strayed from God: they did not accept His Word, imagining they could know God through the Father Himself without the Word, that is to say, without the Son.   IV 7, 4

(75) The precepts given them by Moses for slavery and as a sign have been abolished [by the Lord] through the new convenant of freedom. But the laws which are natural and common to all, the laws befitting free men, He has increased and widened. Lavishly, ungrudgingly, He has granted men to know God the Father through adoption and to love Him wholeheartedly . . . But He has also increased fear, for sons should have more fear and more love for the Father than slaves.   IV 16,5

45

(76) Read the prophets carefully, and you will find that all the actions, all the teaching, all the sufferings of the Lord have been foretold by them. Now it may be that the question will come into your mind: Did the Lord bring us anything new by His coming? The answer is this: He brought us all newness by bringing Himself, who had been foretold. IV 34, 1

(77) He promised to give very much to those who now bear fruit, but through the gift of His grace, not by the changing of our knowledge. For the Lord remains the same, and the same Father is revealed. Thus, by His coming, one and the same Lord has bestowed on those who lived later a greater gift of grace than the one He granted in the old dispensation. IV 11, 3

(78) Everything became new when the Word, in a new dispensation, came in the flesh to win back to God man who had gone off from God. Thus men were taught to worship, not a different God, but the same God in a new way. III 10, 2

1 In this Gnostic myth, Sophia (or Achamoth), the figure of 'Wisdom', appears as the absolute quest, the quest which is an end in itself, The nature of existence is the 'question' here. Irenaeus points out that the Gnostics claim that this insight enables them to grasp the 'nature of existence' , but that means that they are embroiled in a dialectic of (absolute) knowing and (absolute) unknowing. Although this 'tragic dialectic' may assume a Christian disguise, it is in fundamental contradiction to the Gospel of Christ, for which the real search for God is linked with the real finding of God.
2 The number of 'Aeons' in the 'Divine Pleroma'.

Salvation history

In God, the Son is the Word and Image of the Father, and thus the One who makes Him known. It will, therefore, also be the Word of God who shows the Father to the world — just as it is likewise He who shows the world to God — in nature, in grace, and finally by appearing in person Himself.

So all that exists is God's revelation, but that revelation is effected through God's Word. To enable us to see and understand this divine revelation, God the Father in His grace gives us His Holy Spirit.

In the course of history the revelations of the divine Word become increasingly clearer. They move, through the prophecies of the Old Testament, towards the central event, the Incarnation of the Word.

Trinitarian revelation

(79) The [true] Creator is God. In His love He is Father, in His power He is Lord, in His Wisdom He is our maker and fashioner. By transgressing His commandment, we have become His enemies. And so in these last times the Lord has restored us to His friendship by His Incarnation. He became 'the mediator of God and men' (cf 1 Tim. 2:5), pro-pitiating for us the Father against whom we had sinned, consoling Him for our disobedience by His obedience [on the Cross], granting us the grace of conversion and submission to our Creator. He therefore taught us to say in prayer: 'Forgive us our debts' (cf Matt. 6:12), since He is indeed our Father, and we are His debtors, having transgressed His commandment . . . Rightly, then, says the Word to man: 'Your sins are forgiven' (cf Matt. 9:2). The very One against whom we had sinned in the beginning grants remission of sins in the end . . . How can sins truly be forgiven unless

the One against whom we sinned is the very One who has granted forgiveness 'through the tender mercy of our God' (cf Luke 1:78), the mercy in which 'He has visited us' through His Son?

In forgiving sins, the Lord not only healed man, He also showed clearly who He was. If no one can forgive sins but God alone, and if the Lord did forgive them and did heal men, it is plain that He was Himself the Word of God made the Son of Man. Because He was both God and man, He received the power to forgive sins from the Father, so that, since as man He suffered with us, so as God He might take pity on us, and forgive us the debts we owe to God our Creator.   V 17, 1—3

(80) The Spirit of God bestows the knowledge of the truth. In accordance with the Father's will, He is there in each generation to expound the dispensations of the Father and the Son.   IV 33, 7

(81) [The Holy Spirit] therefore descended on the Son of God made the Son of Man. With Him He became accustomed to dwell among the human race, to rest upon men, to inhabit the handiwork of God, accomplishing the Father's will in them, renewing them, taking them from oldness into the newness of Christ . . . The Lord therefore promised to send the Comforter, who would join us to God. Just as dry wheat without moisture cannot make a single mass of dough or a single loaf, so we who are many could not be made one in Christ Jesus without the water from heaven. And just as dry earth, if it does not receive moisture, does not bear fruit, so we, who at first were a dry tree, could never have borne the fruit of life without the free-flowing rain from above.   III 17, 1—2

(82) The dew is the Holy Spirit . . . We need the dew of God to prevent ourselves being consumed by fire.   III 17, 3

(83) Where the Spirit of God is, there is the Church and every grace, but the Spirit is truth. III 24, 1

(84) God is powerful in all things. In the past He was seen prophetically through the Spirit, then He was seen adoptively through the Son, and in the Kingdom of Heaven He will be seen paternally. The Spirit prepares man for the Son of God, the Son leads him to the Father, while the Father confers on him incorruption and eternal life, which comes from the vision of God to those who enjoy it. IV 20, 5

(85) Through all these things God the Father is revealed. The Spirit is at work, the Son carries out His ministry, the Father approves, and man is perfected and brought to salvation. IV 20, 6

Nature, prophecy, incarnation

Universal revelation
(86) 'No one knows the Son except the Father, and no one knows the Father except the Son and anyone to whom the Son chooses to reveal Him' (Matt. 11:27). The word 'reveal' does not have just a future meaning, as if the Word only began to manifest the Father when He was born of Mary; it has a general meeting and applies to the whole of time. From the beginning the Son has been present to His handiwork, and reveals the Father to all, to whom He wills, and when He wills, and as the Father wills. And so in all and through all there is one God the Father and one Word — Son and one Spirit and one salvation for all who believe in Him. IV 6, 7

(87) Through the creation itself the Word reveals God the Creator, and through the world the Lord, the world's Maker, and through the work of art the Artist who fashioned it, and through the Son the Father who begets the

Son . . . Similarly, through the law and the prophets the Word proclaimed both Himself and the Father . . . Finally, through the Word made visible and palpable, the Father was revealed. Though all alike did not believe, all saw the Father in the Son (cf John 14:9), for the Father is the invisible of the Son, and the Son is the visible of the Father. That is why, in His presence, all said that He was Christ and called Him God. The demons, on seeing the Son, said: 'We know who you are . . .' (Mark 1:24). All saw the Son and the Father and called them by those names, but not all believed.   IV 6, 6

The Father revealed in the Son

(88) No one can know the Father without the Word of God, that is to say, unless the Son reveals Him, nor can one know the Son without the good pleasure of the Father (cf Matt. 11:26f). The good pleasure of the Father is carried out by the Son: the Father sends, while the Son is sent and comes. The Father, invisible though He is to us, is known by His own Word, and though inexpressible, the Word expresses Him to us. Again, only the Father knows His Word. Both these truths have been revealed to us by the Lord. Thus the Son reveals the knowledge of the Father by his own manifestation, for the knowledge of the Father is the manifestation of the Son. Everything is manifested through the Word.
                                                                    IV 6, 3

(89) The knowledge of the Father is the Son, but the knowledge of the Son is revealed by the Father through the Son. That is why the Lord said: 'No one knows the Son except the Father, and no one knows the Father except the Son and anyone to whom the Son chooses to reveal Him' (Matt. 11:27).   IV 6, 7

The Son in the Old Testament

(90) The Son of God has been sown everywhere throughout the Scriptures [of Moses]. Sometimes He speaks with

Abraham, sometimes with Noah, giving him the measurements of the ark; He looks for Adam, brings judgement on the Sodomites. There are times when He is actually seen, guiding Jacob on his way, speaking with Moses from the bush.   IV 10, 1

(91) Among the things foretold by the prophets was the prediction that those on whom God's Spirit rested, and who obeyed the Father's Word, and served Him with all their might, would be persecuted, stoned, and put to death. It was out of love for God, and for the sake of His word, that the prophets prefigured all these things in themselves. For they too were members of Christ, and it was in virtue of that membership that each of them set forth his prophecy. Yet, though many, all foretold one person and announced the things pertaining to that one. Just as the functioning of the whole body is manifested by our members, and yet the form of the complete person is not manifested by one member on its own but by all together, so all the prophets as a whole did indeed prefigure the one person [of Christ], while each individual prophet, as a member, fulfilled his role in the total plan and prophesied the particular action of Christ linked with that member.   IV 33, 10

Foreshadowings
(92) The Spirit of God pointed to future things through the prophets in order to prepare and predispose us for submission to God. Now since one of these future things was man's enjoyment, by the good pleasure of the Holy Spirit, of the vision of God, it was necessary that those who announced future things should themselves see the God whom they were intimating men would one day see. The plan was that God and the Son of God, the Father and the Son, should not just be announced prophetically in words, but also be seen by all the members sanctified and instructed in the things of God. Man was to be schooled and made ready for that glory which was later to be revealed to those who love God (cf

Rom. 8:18, 28) . . . It was for this reason, then, that they saw the Son of God as man conversing with men. What was still future, they prophesied; the Person who was not yet there, they said was present. The impassible they proclaimed passible, and Him who then was in heaven they said had descended 'into the dust of death' (cf Ps. 21:16) . . .

The prophets did not, of course, see the face of God unveiled, but only the dispensations and mysteries through which man one day would see God . . . Neither Moses nor Elijah nor Ezekiel saw God, though they did see many heavenly things, things which were 'likenesses of the glory of the Lord' (cf Ezek. 1:28) and prophecies of the future. If this is so, then it is clear that the Father is indeed invisible, of whom the Lord said, 'No one has seen God' (John 1:18). But God's Word, in conformity to His will and for the good of those who saw Him, revealed the glory of the Father and expounded His saving purposes, as the Lord said: 'The only-begotten God, who is in the bosom of the Father, He has made him known' (John 1:18). The Word is the 'exegete' of the Father, and so, since He is richness and multiplicity, He is not seen in just one form or playing one role, but according to the aims and objects of His saving plan . . . Thus the Word of God always showed to men, so to speak, the outlines of the things He was to accomplish in the future, the contours of the Father's saving plan, thereby teaching us the things of God.   IV 20, 8—11

Fulfilment in the flesh

(93) As He reigned in heaven, so the Word of God reigns on earth . . . and He holds sway, too, over the things which are under the earth, having become 'the first-born from the dead' (Col. 1:18), so that, as we have said, all things might behold their King, so that the fatherly light might meet and rest upon the flesh of our Lord, and then, from that resplendent flesh, come upon us, and finally so that man, girded with the fatherly light, might attain to incorruption.
IV 20, 2

Many statements they make sense if
one considers Christ to be united with
the "atomic idea" of a man, participated in by all
others.

Incarnation as Recapitulation

*The prophetic appearances of the Word pointed ahead to the one
mystery: the union of God and man. All the threads in God's saving plan are here entwined. Now the stupendous exchange takes
place: God becomes 'nothing', so that the 'nothings' might
become God, Irenaeus calls this wonderful thing recapitulation
(anakephalaiosis). What he means is this: the second Adam is the
repetition, in divine truth, of the first Adam, the Adam who
turned away from God. The second Adam repeats the whole
natural development of man at the higher level of divine reality.
Sinful, lost, and wandering man is not just put back on course by
the companionship of love; more profoundly, he is taken into that
love.*

*St Paul coined the word 'recapitulation' to express the mean-
ing of the Incarnation: it was God's plan to 'bring everything
together under Christ as Head, everything in the heavens and
everything on earth' (Eph. 1:10, Jerusalem Bible translation). As
recapitulation (ana-kephalaiosis), Christ is the Head (caput,
kephale) of the world.*

*In Him everything becomes clear and has meaning: the 'sal-
vific order of sin', which makes possible the revelation of God's
superbundant mercy (Irenaeus here puts forward his boldest
ideas); the self-abasement of Christ, by which He gets down to
man and lifts him up to God; the reconciliation of the world and
God, of nature and grace, which has its foundation in the one
Incarnation.*

*This indestructible interweaving of things is the true touch-
stone of what is Catholic. The Gnostics tear Christ into two
pieces; a mortal man and a spiritual being incapable of suffering;
in so doing, they disown the heart of Christianity. Only when
matter, Christ's very body, is safeguarded in God, is man
redeemed. That is why Irenaeus regards the Eucharist as the
pledge of redemption: here the fruit of the dark earth itself is
transformed into grace.*

The exchange between God and man

(94) The Son of God became the Son of Man, so that through Him we might receive adoption. This takes place when man receives and bears and embraces the Son of God.   III 16, 3

(95) He became the Son of Man to accustom man to receive God and God to dwell in man.   III 20, 2

(96) In His immeasurable love, He became what we are in order to make us what He is.   V, preface

(97) The proclamation of the Church alone is true, namely, that God's own creation, which depends for its existence on God's power and art and wisdom, has borne God. In an invisible way, the creation is borne by the Father, but in a visible way, it does indeed bear the Word. And this is the truth.   V 18, 1

(98) Spiritual though it was (cf Rom. 7:14), the law only manifested sin; it did not suppress it, for sin did not hold sway just over the spirit, but over the [whole] man. It was necessary, therefore, that the One who came to slay sin, and to redeem man deserving of death, should become precisely what man is, namely, man. It was man who was dragged by sin into slavery and held fast by death, and so it had to be a man by whom sin was slain, a man who went forth from death.   III 18, 7

(99) [In this way] He attached and united man to God. Had man not vanquished the enemy of man, the enemy would not have been justly vanquished. On the other hand, had it not been God who granted salvation, we could never have possessed it securely. And if man had not been united to

God, he could never have become a partaker of incorruptibility. It required the Mediator of God and men, through His kinship with both, to bring back both to friendship and concord, presenting man to God, revealing God to man.

III 18, 7

(100) There was no other way for us to receive incorruptibility and immortality than to be united to incorruptibility and immortality. But how could we be united to incorruptibility and immortality without incorruptibility and immortality first becoming what we are, the perishable putting on imperishability, the mortal putting on immortality (cf 1 Cor. 15:54), 'so that we might receive adoption as sons' (Gal. 4:5)?

III 19, 1

Creation in Christ

Heaven and earth united in Christ
(101) Into the paradise of life the Lord leads those who obey His preaching, 'recapitulating all things in Himself, things in heaven and things on earth' (cf Eph. 1:10). 'Things in heaven' are those which are spiritual, while the phrase 'things on earth' refers to that work of God which is man. Both these He has recapitulated in Himself, uniting man to the Spirit and making the Spirit to dwell in man. He became the head[1] of the Spirit and gave the Spirit to be the head of man, for it is by the Spirit that we see and hear and speak.

V 20, 2

Created spirit and uncreated Spirit
(102) The Father bears the creation and His Word simultaneously, and the Word borne by the Father bestows the Spirit on all as the Father wills. To some, in the order of creation, He gives the spirit belonging to creation, the spirit that is created. To others, in the order of adoption, He gives the Spirit who comes from the Father, the Spirit brought

forth by Him.[2] And thus one God the Father is revealed, 'who is above all and through all and in all' (Eph. 4:6). The Father is above all, and He is the head of Christ (cf 1 Cor. 11:3). But the Word is through all, and He is the head of the Church (cf Eph. 5:23). And the Spirit is in all, and He is the living water, which the Lord grants to those who believe rightly in Him and love Him and know that there is one Father, 'who is above all and through all and in all'.

V 18, 2

Through the Incarnation the image of God is shown forth

(103) The truth of this was shown when the Word of God became man, assimilating Himself to man and man to Himself, so that, by His resemblance to the Son, man might become precious to the Father. For in times past it was *said* that man was made in the image of God, but not *shown*, because the Word, in whose image man was made, was still invisible. That is why man lost the likeness so easily. But when the Word of God was made flesh, He confirmed both things: He showed the true image, when He Himself became what His image was; and He restored and made fast the likeness, making man like the invisible Father through the visible Word. V 16, 2

Man brought back by persuasion, not violence

(104) Apostasy reigned over us unjustly, and, though by nature we belonged to almighty God, it alienated us against our nature, making us its own disciples. And so, in all things mighty, in His justice indefectible, the Word of God turned justly against this apostasy, redeeming from it His own property. He did not use violence, as the apostasy had done at the beginning when it usurped dominion over us, greedily snatching what was not its own. No, He used persuasion. It was fitting for God to use persuasion, not violence, to obtain what He wanted, so that justice should not be infringed and God's ancient handiwork not be utterly destroyed. V 1, 1

The Incarnation of the Word fulfils God's first plan

(105) [The Gnostics] reject the commixture of the heavenly wine. They only want to be the water of this world and will not admit God into commixture with them.[3] And so they remain in the Adam conquered and cast out of Paradise. They fail to see that, as at the beginning of our formation in Adam the breath of life which comes from God was united to what had been formed, animated man, and showed him to be a rational animal, so, at the end, the Word of the Father and the Spirit of God, united to the ancient substance of Adam's formation, made man living and perfect, capable of knowing the perfect Father. This was so that, as in the 'animal man' we all die, so in the 'spiritual man' we might all be made alive (cf 1 Cor. 15:22). Adam at no time escaped the Hands of God [the Son and the Spirit], to whom the Father said, 'Let us make man in our image and likeness' (Gen. 1:26). That is why, at the end, 'not by the will of the flesh or the will of a man', but by the good pleasure of the Father, the Hands of God made the living Man, so that Adam might come into the image and likeness of God. V 1, 3

Our Teacher had to become visible to us

(106) There was no other way by which we could learn the things of God than for our Teacher, who is the Word, to become man. No other could have revealed to us the secrets of the Father, none but the Father's very own Word. 'For who (else) has known the mind of the Lord, or who has been His counsellor?' (cf Rom. 11:34). Again, there was no other way for us to learn than to see our Teacher and hear His voice with our own ears. It is by becoming imitators of His actions and doers of His words that we have communion with Him. It is from Him who has been perfect from before all creation that we, so lately made, receive fulfilment.   V 1, 1

The only definitive thing is the Incarnation

(107) Vain indeed are those who claim that He only

seemed to appear. These things took place in actual reality, not in mere imagination. If He had appeared as man without actually being man, He would not have remained what in truth He was, the spiritual reality that is God, for the spiritual is invisible. Nor would the truth have been in Him, because He would not have been what He seemed to be.

We said earlier that Abraham and the other prophets saw Him prophetically; by vision, they prophesied what was to come. If He had now appeared in that way, not being what He seemed to be, He would have given a kind of prophetic vision to men; we would then have to await another coming of this same Lord, in which He would be exactly what He had then been seen prophetically to be. V 1, 2

(108) If the Lord had become incarnate in some other dispensation and taken flesh from another substance, He would not have recapitulated man in Himself. In fact, one could not then really use the word 'flesh', because the flesh is in continuity with the first fashioning of man, when he was made from the dust of the earth. Had it been necessary for Him to have matter from another substance, the Father, at the very beginning, would have used another substance to mould His handiwork. In fact, the saving Word made Himself precisely what lost man was, by His own act bringing man into communion with Himself and obtaining man's salvation. Now what was lost had flesh and blood. For man was fashioned by God from the dust of the earth, and for the sake of man the whole dispensation of the Lord's coming took place. He too, therefore, had flesh and blood, recapitulating in Himself not something else, but that original handiwork of the Father, 'seeking [and saving] the lost' (cf Luke 19:10). V 14, 2

(109) What He appeared to be, He really was. God recapitulated in Himself that ancient handiwork of His which is man, in order to kill sin, to destroy death, and to give life to man. These are His true works. III 18, 7

(110) When He became incarnate and was made man, He recapitulated in Himself the long history of mankind and, in that summing up, procured for us the salvation we lost in Adam.   III 13, 1

In the flesh the Word works by silence

(111) Just as He was man in order to be tempted, so He was Word to be glorified. The Word went [so to speak] into 're-pose', so that He could be tempted, dishonoured, crucified, and put to death, while the manhood [in its natural weak-ness] was 'absorbed' [into the infinite power of the Word] when the Lord conquered, endured, rose again, and ascended.[4]   III 19, 3

(112) Scripture says that Christ, though He is God and spiritual, had to become a man capable of suffering. The Bible is, as it were, astonished at His sufferings, amazed that the One under whose 'shadow we said we wanted to dwell' should have to endure such agonies. By 'shadow' Scripture here means His body. For just as a shadow is made by the body, so the body of Christ is made by His Spirit. But He also indicates the lowliness of His body and the contempt to which it was subjected by this word 'shadow', in the sense that just as the shadow of an upright body lies on the ground and is trodden on, so the body of Christ was thrown to the ground and, as it were, trampled underfoot in His Passion. Finally, Scripture calls Christ's body a 'shadow' because it shaded and enfolded the glory of the Spirit. People plagued with all kinds of illnesses were often laid in the street as Jesus passed by, and those touched by His shadow were healed.   D 71

(113) How could we be partakers of adoption as God's sons without receiving from Him, through the Son, the gift of communion with Him? . . . This is why He passed through all the ages of human life, restoring to all men communion with God.   III 18, 7

59

The mystery of the Virgin

(114) The first formed man, Adam, received his substance from the untilled and still virgin earth ('for God had not caused it to rain upon the earth, and there was no man to till the ground', Gen. 2:5) and was fashioned by the Hand of God, that is, the Word of God (for 'all things were made through Him', John 1:3, and 'God took dust from the earth and formed man', Gen. 2:7). Similarly, the Word, recapitulating Adam in Himself, very fittingly received from Mary, who was still a virgin, the birth which made recapitulation possible . . . Why did God not take dust again? Why did He make the formation come from Mary? Precisely so that there was not some different formation, that it was not some different handiwork which was saved, that it was the very same one which was recapitulated, the likeness being preserved.   III 21, 10

(115) [The prophets] who proclaimed Him as Emmanuel, born of the Virgin, were showing forth the union of the Word of God with His own handiwork. They were announcing that the Word would be made flesh, that the Son of God would become the Son of Man, that the Pure One, in a pure way, would open that pure womb which regenerates men in God, that pure womb which He Himself made to be pure.   IV 33, 11

(116) Consequently, the Virgin Mary is found to be obedient, when she says, 'Behold the handmaid of the Lord. Be it done unto me according to thy word' (Luke 1:38). Eve was disobedient; while still a virgin, she did not obey. She had Adam for a husband, but she was nonetheless still a virgin, for in Paradise 'they were both naked and not ashamed' (Gen. 2:25). The reason for this was that they had only been created a short time before and so had no understanding of the procreation of children. They had

first of all to grow up; only then could they multiply. Just as Eve, by disobeying, became the cause of death for herself and the whole human race, so Mary, betrothed to a predestined man and yet a virgin, by obeying, became the cause of salvation for herself and the whole human race. This is why the law gives the name 'wife' to a woman who is betrothed to a man but still a virgin, thereby indicating the circular movement from Mary back to Eve. What was bound could not be untied without a reversal of the process of entanglement. The first bonds had to be untied by the second, so that the second might set free the first. And, in fact, this is what happened: the first entanglement was untied by the second bond, the second bond playing the role of loosener of the first. This is why the Lord said that the first would be last and the last first (cf Matt. 19:30; 20:16). And the prophet made the same point when he said: 'Instead of fathers sons shall be born to you' (Ps. 44:17). For the Lord, born as 'the first-born from the dead' (Col. 1:18), took to His bosom the ancient 'fathers' and regenerated them into the life of God. He became the beginning of those who live, as Adam had been the beginning of those who die. St Luke, therefore, begins his genealogy with the Lord and then takes it back to Adam, thereby showing that it was not the fathers who gave life to the Lord but the Lord who gave them rebirth in the Gospel of life. Similarly, the knot of Eve's disobedience was untied through the obedience of Mary. For what the virgin Eve tied through unbelief, the Virgin Mary set free through faith.   III 22, 4

The recapitulation of suffering

Only real flesh suffers
(117) Had He received nothing from Mary [as the Gnostics believe], He would never have taken the foods which come from the earth, the foods by which the body taken from the earth is nourished. Nor would He have felt hunger after

fasting, like Moses and Elijah, for forty days, if His body had not been seeking its proper nourishment. Nor would John his disciple have written: 'Jesus, wearied by the journey, sat down' (John 4:6), nor would David have prophesied of Him: 'They added to the pain of my wounds' (cf Ps. 68:27). Nor would He have wept over Lazarus, nor would He have sweated drops of blood, nor would blood and water have flowed from His pierced side. For these are all signs of flesh taken from the earth, the flesh which the Lord recapitulated in Himself, in order to save His own handiwork.   III 22, 2

Real blood must flow if there is to be redemption

(118) Were it not a question of saving the flesh, the Word of God would not have been made flesh, and if the blood of the just had not required a reckoning, He would certainly not have had blood. But, in fact, from the beginning the blood of the just has had a voice. God said to Cain when he had killed his brother: 'The voice of your brother's blood is crying to me' (Gen. 4:10). And since He required a reckoning for their blood, He said to those with Noah: 'For your lifeblood I will surely require a reckoning; of every beast I will require it' (Gen. 9:5). And again: 'Whoever sheds the blood of man, by man shall his blood be shed' (Gen. 9:6). Similarly, the Lord said to those who were to shed His blood: 'All the just blood shed upon earth will be required, from the blood of just Abel to the blood of Zechariah, the son of Barachiah, whom you murdered between the temple and the altar. Truly I say to you, all this will come upon this generation' (cf Matt. 23:35—36; Luke 11:50—51). In saying this, He is pointing to the coming recapitulation in Himself of the blood shed by the prophets and all the just from the beginning; He is pointing to the 'requiring' of their blood in Himself. Now this blood would not have been required unless it had the capability of being saved. Nor would the Lord have recapitulated all this in Himself if He had not been made flesh and blood in conformity to the original

handiwork. In the end he saved in Himself what in the beginning had perished in Adam. V 14, 1

The meaning of history

Everything takes place at its appointed time

(119) [The heretics] err from the truth, because their doctrine is far removed from the true God. They are ignorant of the fact that His only-begotten Word, who has always been present to the human race, and who, by the Father's good pleasure, has been united and mingled with His own handiwork and made flesh, is our Lord Jesus Christ, who suffered for us, rose again for us, and will come again in the glory of the Father to resurrect all flesh, to manifest salvation, and to apply the rule of just judgement to all submitted to Him.

There is one God the Father . . . and one Jesus Christ our Lord, who came by means of this whole dispensation, recapitulating all things in Himself. Now this 'all' includes man, the handiwork of God, and so He recapitulated man in Himself, the invisible becoming visible, the incomprehensible becoming comprehensible, the impassible becoming passible, the Word becoming man. He recapitulated all things in Himself, so that, as the Word of God rules over the supercelestial, spiritual, and invisible, so He has primacy over the visible and corporeal. Appropriating the primacy and appointing Himself Head of the Church, He draws all things to Himself (cf John 12:32) at the proper time.

With Him, there is nothing out of keeping, nothing out of season, just as with the Father there is nothing incongruous. For all things have been foreknown by the Father and accomplished by the Son in the way and at the time decreed. This is why, when Mary urged Him to perform the miraculous sign of the wine and wanted to partake, before the time, of the cup of recapitulation,[5] the Lord checked her untimely haste and said: 'O woman, what have you to do with me? My hour has not yet come' (John 2:4). He was waiting for the hour foreknown by the Father . . . It is clear, then, that everything foreknown by the Father was accomplished by our Lord in the fitting order and at the foreknown time and hour. He is one and the same Lord, but rich and multiple.   III 16, 6—7

Christ the Saviour forms Adam with Himself in view

(120) He recapitulates in Himself all the nations dispersed since Adam, and all the languages and generations of men, including Adam himself. This is why St Paul calls Adam the 'type of the One who was to come' (cf Rom. 5:14), because the Word, the maker of all things, did a preliminary sketch in Adam of what, in God's plan, was to come to the human race through the Son of God. God arranged it so that the first man was animal in nature and saved by the spiritual Man. Since the Saviour existed already, the one to be saved had to be brought into existence, so that the Saviour should not be in vain.   III 22, 3

The old covenant as man's preparation for Christ

(121) At the beginning, God, out of His generosity, formed man. For their salvation, He chose the patriarchs. And to teach the ignorant to follow God, He formed a people in advance . . . He thus accustomed man to bear His Spirit and to live in communion with God. He Himself needed no one, but He bestowed communion with Himself on those who needed Him. For those who were pleasing to Him, He sketched, like an architect, the plan of salvation. In Egypt, to those who could not see Him, He gave Himself as guide. In the desert, to the restless, He gave a most suitable law. In the promised land, to those who entered, He supplied a noble inheritance. For those who returned to the Father, He killed the fatted calf and presented them with the finest robe (cf Luke 15:22—23). In all these different ways, He pre-

pared mankind for the harmonious music of salvation (cf Luke 15:25). St John therefore says in the Apocalypse: 'His voice was like the sound of many waters' (Apoc. 1:15). Yes, the waters of God's Spirit are many, for rich and great is the Father. And at every stage the Word ungrudgingly gives His assistance to those subject to Him by drawing up a law adapted and appropriate to every creature. IV 14, 2

(122) The giving of the law had to come to an end when the new covenant was revealed. For God does everything in measure and order; with him, there is nothing unmeasured, because there is nothing disordered. He spoke well who said that the immeasurable Father is measured in the Son, because the Son is the measure of the Father; He comprehends Him.   IV 4, 2

The meaning of creatureliness

(123) This is what distinguishes God from man: God makes, man is made. The Maker is always the same, while what is made has to have a beginning, a middle, and a final state of maturity. God makes well, man is well made. God is perfect in everything, like and equal to Himself, wholly light, wholly mind, wholly substance, the fount of all good, whereas man receives increase and progress towards God. Just as God is always the same, so man in God always makes progress towards God. God never ceases to benefit and enrich man, and man never ceases to receive the benefit and enrichment from God.   IV 11, 2

(124) God is uncreated, without beginning or end, in need of nothing, and the existence of all other things is His gift to them. Everything made by Him has received a beginning, and everything with a beginning is liable to dissolution, is subject to, and in need of, the One who created it.

III 83, 3

(125) Someone may at this stage raise this objection: 'Could God not have created man perfect from the beginning?' To this we must answer that, for God, who as regards Himself is uncreated and always identical with Himself, all things are possible. But the things He created come into existence later; their createdness has a beginning; and so they are of necessity inferior to the One who made them. The newly created cannot be uncreated. They are not uncreated, and so they fall short of perfection. Being younger, they are little children, and as little children, they are unaccustomed to and unskilled in perfect discipline. A mother *could* give her child grown-up food, but she does not, because the child is still incapable of receiving stronger nourishment. Similarly, God had the power to give man perfection from the beginning, but man was incapable of receiving it, because he was an infant. This is why our Lord came to us in these last times, recapitulating all things in Himself, not as He might have done, but as we were capable of beholding Him. He could have come to us in His indescribable glory, but we could not have endured the greatness of that glory. Therefore, as if to infants, the perfect Bread of the Father gave Himself to us as milk . . . He nourished us at the breast of His flesh, a suckling which was to prepare us for eating and drinking the Word of God. All this was to enable us to contain within ourselves the bread of immortality, which is the Spirit of the Father.

IV 38, 1

(126) It was for this reason that the Word of God, though perfect, became a child in solidarity with mankind. He did not do this for His own sake but because of the state of childhood in which man then existed. He wanted to be received in a way that suited man's capacity to receive.

IV 38, 2

(127) God's power and wisdom and goodness are displayed simultaneously. He reveals His power and

goodness by creating and establishing, by His own free will, things which have no previous existence. He manifests His wisdom by making things part of one coherent and harmonious whole. His creatures, given, by His immeasurable kindness, increase and continued existence through the length of days, show forth the glory of the Uncreated, of the God who ungrudgingly gives what is good. As created, they are not uncreated, but as continuing in existence through long ages, they receive something of the power of the Uncreated; their permanent existence is God's gratuitous gift. Thus God will have the primacy in all things, since He alone is uncreated and before all things; He causes everything to be. All other things remain in subjection to God. But subjection to God is incorruptibility, and the permanence of incorruptibility is the glory of the Uncreated. This is the order, this is the rhythm, this is the movement by which man, that created and organized being, is established in the image and likeness of the uncreated God. The Father, in His good pleasure, commands, the Son works and fashions, the Spirit nourishes and gives increase, and slowly but surely man makes progress and attains perfection, that is to say, comes close to the Uncreated. For the perfect is uncreated, and the uncreated is God. Thus man had first to be made, once made to grow, once grown to become an adult, once adult to multiply, once multiplied to grow strong, once strong to be glorified, and once glorified to see His Lord. For it is God whom one day we shall see, and the vision of God procures immortality, and 'immortality brings one near to God' (Wisd. 6:19).   IV 38, 3

The meaning of sin

(128) It is, therefore, totally unreasonable when people refuse to await the time of growth, and ascribe the frailty of their nature to God. They know neither God nor

themselves. They are insatiable and ungrateful, unwilling to be at the outset what they were made to be, human beings subject to passions. Passing beyond the law of the human race, they want, before becoming men, to be like God the Creator and abolish the difference between uncreated God and recently made man. They are more stupid than dumb animals, for they after all do not reproach God for not having made them men, but each gives thanks for being made what it has been made. We, by contrast, blame God because He has not made us gods from the beginning, but first men and then gods later . . .

In His generosity, He has bestowed the good and made man in His likeness, endowed with free will. By His foreknowledge, He knew the frailty of man and what would result from it, but in His love and power, He will triumph over the substance of created nature. It was necessary that, first, nature appeared, then that the mortal was conquered and swallowed up by immortality, the corruptible by incorruptibility, and that man should be made in the image and likeness of God, having received the knowledge of good and evil.   IV 38, 4—5

(129) Man has received the knowledge of good and evil. Now it is good to obey God, to believe in Him, and to keep His commandments; that is the life of man. And it is evil not to obey God; that is the death of man. Through the magnanimity which God gave him, man has known both the good of obedience and the evil of disobedience, so that the eye of his mind, having experienced both, might with discernment choose the better, and be neither slothful nor neglectful of the commandment of God. He learns from experience that disobeying God, which robs him of life, is evil, and so he never attempts it . . . Thus he has a twofold faculty for knowing the two, to enable him to choose the better with discernment. But how could he have discerned the good without knowing its opposite? For first-hand experience is more certain and reliable than conjecture. The

tongue experiences sweet and bitter by taste, the eye distinguishes black from white by sight, and the ear perceives different sounds by hearing. Similarly, the mind acquires the knowledge of the good through the experience of both, and becomes more firmly committed to preserving it by obeying God. First, by penance, he rejects disobedience, because it is bitter and evil. Then he realizes what it really is — the opposite of goodness and sweetness, and so he is never tempted to taste disobedience to God. But if you repudiate this knowledge of both, this twofold faculty of discernment, unwittingly you destroy your humanity.   IV 39, 1

God showed forbearance when man apostasized, because He foresaw the victory which one day would be given Him through the Word. For when 'power was made perfect in weakness' (cf 2 Cor. 12:9), the Word revealed God's loving kindness and His magnificent power. Man can be compared to the prophet Jonah. God allowed him to be swallowed by a sea monster, not so he should be devoured and totally perish, but so that, having been vomited out, he might be more submitted to God and glorify Him more . . . In the same way, at the beginning, God permitted man to be swallowed by the great monster who was the author of transgression. He did not want man to be devoured and utterly destroyed; He was simply premeditating and preparing the gaining of salvation by the Word through 'the sign of Jonah' (cf Matt. 12:39f) for the benefit of those who think of God as Jonah did and confess . . . 'I cried to the Lord my God in my distress, and He heard me from the belly of hell' (Jonah 2:2). God wanted man to go on glorifying Him for ever and to give thanks unceasingly for the salvation received from Him, 'so that no flesh should glory in His presence' (1 Cor. 1:29). He did not want man ever to go astray in his thinking about God, by imagining the incorruptibility he enjoys to be a natural property, and by boasting in vanity and conceit, in abrogation of the truth, as if he were naturally like God. Such pride increased man's ingratitude to his Creator, obscured God's love for him, and blinded his mind. It prevented him from thinking worthily about God, and led him to compare himself with God, judging himself to be God's equal.

This, then, was the forbearance of God. He permitted man to pass through every situation, to undergo death, and then to come to the resurrection of the dead, discovering from experience the evil from which he had been delivered. Thus man will for ever give thanks to the Lord for the gift of incorruptibility, and will love Him more, for the one to whom more is forgiven loves more (cf Luke 7:42f). He will recognize that he himself is mortal and weak, and that God, by contrast, is immortal and so mighty that He can give immortality to the mortal and eternity to the temporal. He will also have an insight into the other divine attributes he has been shown; these will teach him to have thoughts about God that are worthy of God. For the glory of man is God, and the receptacle of God's work and wisdom and power is man. Just as a doctor proves himself among the sick, so God manifests Himself among men. As St Paul says, 'God has shut up all things in unbelief, that He may have mercy on all' (Rom. 11:32).   III 20, 1—2

(130) Things which fall into our lap and things acquired after much effort are not cherished in the same way. Now we were called to love God more, and that, according to what the Lord taught and the apostle handed on, involves struggle. Were this not so, we would not appreciate the good; where there is no exertion, there is no appreciation. Sight would not be so desirable if we did not know what a great evil blindness is. Health, too, is made more precious by the experience of sickness; light by comparison with darkness; life with death. In the same way, the heavenly kingdom is more precious to those who have known the earthly one. But the more precious it is, the more we love it;

and the more we love it, the more glorious shall we be in the presence of God. God, therefore, permitted all these things, so that we, instructed by them all, might in future be prudent in all things, and, wisely taught to love God, might abide in that perfect love (cf John 15:9f). God showed forbearance at the apostasy of man, and man learnt from it, as the prophet says: 'Your apostasy will instruct you' (Jer. 2:19). Thus God planned everything in advance for the perfection of man, and for the realization and revelation of His dispensations, that His goodness might be displayed, His justice fulfilled, the Church conformed to the image of His Son (cf Rom. 8:29), and that man might one day be mature, mature enough to see and understand God.

IV 37, 7

(131) How could man have ever known that he was weak and mortal by nature, whereas God was immortal and mighty, if he had not had experience of both? To discover his weakness through suffering is not in any sense evil; on the contrary, it is good not to have an erroneous view of one's own nature. But when man rises up against God, when he is presumptuous and glorifies himself, he becomes ungrateful and does himself great harm, depriving himself both of truth and of love for his Creator. However, the experience of both [good and evil] has produced in man the true knowledge of God and of man, and increased his love for God. And where there is an increase of love, a greater glory is procured by God's power for those who love Him.   V 3, 1

(132) [Those who deny the freedom of the will] present to us a powerless Lord, as if He were incapable of doing what He wants . . . They say that He should not have created angels capable of transgression or human beings who would immediately become ungrateful to Him. These are rational beings, endowed with the power of examining and judging. They are not like irrational or inanimate creatures,

which can do nothing by their own will, but are attracted to the good by necessity and constraint. In these creatures there is only one tendency and one behaviour, inflexible and without judgement; they cannot be anything other than what they were made to be.

Now, on this supposition, the good would have no charm for men, nor would communion with God be precious. If the good were attainable without movement, interest, or application, produced mechanically and without effort, it would have no great appeal. Good things would have no superiority, since they would be good by nature rather than by will; they would possess goodness mechanically rather than by free choice, and so would never know the beauty of the good and would never delight in it. IV 37, 6

Patient maturing

(133) How can you be a god when you have not yet become a man? How can you be perfect when you have only just been made? How can you be immortal when, in your mortal nature, you do not obey your Maker? You must hold the rank of man before you partake of the glory of God. You did not make God; God made you. If you are the handiwork of God, await the Craftsman's hand patiently; He does everything at a favourable time, favourable, that is, to you, whom He made. Offer him your heart, pliant and unresisting. Preserve the form in which the Craftsman fashioned you. Keep within you the Water which comes from Him; without it, you harden and lose the imprint of His fingers. By preserving the structure, you will ascend to perfection; God's artistry will conceal the clay within you. His hand formed your substance; He will coat you, within and without, in pure gold and silver; He will adorn you so well that 'the King Himself will delight in your beauty' (Ps. 44:12). But if you harden and reject His artistry, if you show

Him your displeasure at being made a man, your ingratitude to God will lose you both His artistry and His life.
Making is a property of God's generosity; being made is a
property of man's nature. If, therefore, you hand over to
Him what is yours, faith in Him and subjection to Him, you
will receive the benefit of His artistry and be God's perfect
work of art. If, on the other hand, you resist Him and flee
from His hands, the cause of your imperfection will lie in
you . . . The light does not fail because of those who have
blinded themselves; it remains the same, while the blinded
are plunged in darkness by their own fault. Light never
forces itself on anyone, nor does God use compulsion on
anyone who refuses to accept His artistry.   IV 39, 2—3

Continuity and discontinuity in salvation history

The New Testament hidden in the Old
(134) The new covenant was known and proclaimed by the
prophets, and the One who, by the Father's good pleasure,
was to establish it was proclaimed by them. He was
manifested to men in the way that God willed, so that those
who believe in Him might always make progress and grow,
through the Testaments, into the perfection of salvation.
For there is only one salvation and one God, but the
precepts for forming man are many, and the steps leading
him to God are not a few. An earthly and temporal king,
though he is just a man, is allowed frequently to grant his
subjects great favours. Is it not, then, lawful for God, who is
eternally the same, to grant the human race ever greater
grace and honour those who please with ever richer gifts?
IV 9, 3

(135) The writings of Moses are Christ's own words. He
shows this Himself when He says to the Jews, according to

the testimony of John: 'If you believed Moses, you would believe me, for he wrote of me. But if you do not believe his writings, how will you believe my words?' (John 5:46f). He makes it abundantly clear that the writings of Moses are His own words.   IV 2, 3

(136) All things are thus of one and the same substance; in other words, they come from one and the same God. As the Lord says to His disciples, 'Every scribe who has been trained for the kindgom of heaven is like a householder who brings out of his treasure what is new and what is old' (Matt. 13:52). He did not say that the one who brought out the old and the one who brought out the new were two different people; no, one and the same person brings out both. For the householder is the Lord, who has authority over the whole paternal house. He draws up an appropriate law for slaves who are still untrained, gives suitable precepts to those who are free and justified by faith, and opens up his inheritance to those who are sons . . . The things 'new and old' which He brings out of his treasure are, without doubt, the two Testaments: the old are the earlier giving of the law, the new are life according to the Gospel. As David says, 'Sing to the Lord a new song' (Ps. 95:1; 97:1) . . . The two testaments have been brought forth by one and the same householder, the Word of God, our Lord Jesus Christ, who spoke with Abraham and Moses. And it is He who has restored us anew to freedom, and multiplied the grace which comes from Him.

'Something greater than the temple', He says, 'is here' (Matt. 12:6). Now the words 'greater' or 'less' cannot be applied to things which have nothing in common, which are of an opposite nature and in conflict with each other, but rather to things which are of the same substance, which have something in common, differing from each other only in quantity and magnitude, for example, water from water, light from light, grace from grace.   IV 9, 1—3

(137) Through secondary things He called the people's attention to what was primary, that is to say, through the figurative to the true. IV 14, 3

(138) 'For Christ is the end of the law, that everyone who has faith may be justified' (Rom. 10:4). How could Christ be the end of the law if He were not its beginning? For the one who brought in the end carried out the beginning.

IV 12, 4

(139) The people received all these gifts, oblations, and sacrifices as figures, as was shown to Moses on the mountain by one and the same God, whose name is now glorified in the Church among all the nations. It is fitting that earthly things, which are ordered towards us, should be types of the heavenly, both being made by the same God. No one else could have made the earthly the image of the heavenly. IV 19, 1

The commandment of love was already contained within the law
(140) The tradition of their elders, which they claimed to observe as equal to the Law, was contrary to the Law given by Moses. That is why Isaiah said: 'Your tavern-keepers mix water with wine' (Is. 1:22). What he meant was that the elders were in the habit of mixing the water of tradition with the full-bodied commandment of God. In other words, they set up an adulterated law, a law opposed to the true Law. The Lord made this clear to them when He said: 'Why do you transgress the commandment of God for the sake of your tradition?' (Matt. 15:3). Not content with violating God's law by their transgression, by their mixing wine with water, they have set up against it their own law, the law still called today the 'Pharisaical law'. Some things in the Law they suppress, other things they add, others they interpret as they will, a method which their teachers exploit, each one in his own way. By trying to defend their traditions, they have failed to submit themselves to the

Law of God, which prepares them for the coming of Christ. They even reproached the Lord for healing on the sabbath, which the Law did not forbid . . . But they did not reproach themselves for transgressing God's commandment by their tradition and . . . Pharisaical law, and for not having the principal thing in the Law, namely, love for God.

For this is the first and greatest commandment, and the second is love of neighbour; on these commandments, as the Lord said, hang all the law and the prophets (cf Matt. 22:37—40). And He Himself did not bring any commandment greater than this one; He simply renewed it, commanding His disciples to love God with their whole heart and their neighbour as themselves. If He had descended from a different Father, He would never have made use of the first and greatest commandment of the law; He would have strived in every way possible to bring down a greater commandment than this from the 'perfect Father', so as not to use the one given by the 'God of the law'. But, as St Paul says, 'love is the fulfilling of the law' (Rom. 13:10) . . .

The founder of the Law and the Gospel is shown to be one and the same. The commandments of the perfect life are the same in the two Testaments and point to the same Lord. True, He promulgated particular precepts appropriate to each, but the highest and most excellent, without which one cannot be saved, He proposed in both Testaments.   IV 12, 1—3

(141) All these [commandments of Christ] contain no contradiction to those which preceded them, nor do they abolish them, as Marcion's followers loudly allege; no, they fulfil and extend them . . . For since the Law was imposed on slaves, it educated the soul by means of external and corporeal things, so that man, led to obey the commandments by, as it were, a chain, might learn to say Yes to God. But the Word set the soul free, and showed by His teaching how the body, through the soul, could be purified

in a voluntary way. Once this was accomplished, the chains of slavery to which man had become accustomed had to be removed; now he had to serve God without chains. But, at the same time, the laws of liberty were extended, and submission to the King was increased, so that no one should turn back and and show himself unworthy of his Liberator. Devotion and obedience to the Master of the house were to be the same among both slaves and free men, but he wanted the trust of the sons to be greater, for the working of freedom is greater and more glorious than the docility of slavery. That is why, in place of the commandment 'You shall not commit adultery', He says 'You shall not lust' (cf Matt. 5:27f). In place of 'You shall not kill', 'You shall not even be angry' (cf Matt. 5:21f) . . . 'And if anyone forces you', He says, 'to go one mile, go with him two miles' (Matt. 5:41), so that you do not follow him as a slave but go before him as a free man . . . As we have said, all this could not be said by someone who was abolishing the Law, but by the One who came to fulfil, extend, and widen it among us. You might say that the greater working of liberty implies a more complete and deeply rooted submission and devotion to our Liberator. For He did not liberate us in order to detach us from Himself (after all, no one, outside the good things of the Lord, can procure the food of salvation for himself). No, the idea was that, the more we receive His grace, the more we should love Him, and the more we love Him, the greater the glory we receive from Him when we are for ever in the sight of the Father. IV 13, 1—3

The Church

(142) He fulfilled all things by His coming, and still, in the Church, to the final consummation, He fulfils the new covenant foretold by the Law. IV 34, 2

The choice of the harlot

(143) Hosea the prophet, therefore, took 'a wife of harlotry'. The prophetic significance of this action was that the earth — in other words, the human beings who live on earth — was committing great harlotry by forsaking the Lord (cf Hos. 1:2). From these human beings it would please God to form the Church, who would be sanctified by her union with the Son of God, as the woman was by her union with the prophet. For this reason, too, St Paul said that 'the unbelieving wife is sanctified through her husband' (cf 1 Cor. 7:14) . . . What the prophet did by way of type has been shown by the apostle to have been done in reality in the Church by Christ. Thus Moses took an Ethiopian woman as his wife . . . which signifies the Church taken from among the Gentiles. Those who disparage, criticize, and mock her will not be pure; they will be leprous and cast out of the camp (cf Num. 12:10—14). Rahab the harlot, who accused herself of being a Gentile guilty of every sin, nonetheless welcomed the three spies who went to view all the land and hid them in her house (the three were a type of the Father and the Son with the Holy Spirit) (Josh. 2:1ff). And when the whole town where she lived fell into ruins at the sound of the seven trumpets, Rahab the harlot, with her whole household, was saved by faith in the scarlet sign (cf Josh. 2:18). As the Lord said to the Pharisees, who did not welcome Him when He came and despised that scarlet sign which was the Pasch, the ransom and exodus of the people from Egypt: 'The tax-collectors and harlots go into the kingdom of God before you' (Matt. 21:31).

IV 20, 12

Christ hands over the Truth that He is to the Apostles. They in turn proclaim it orally and in writing and hand it over to the successors publicly instituted by them.

(144) The Lord of all gave to His apostles the power to preach the Gospel. It is through them that we have come to know the truth, that is, the doctrine of the Son of God. The

Lord says to them: 'He who hears you hears me, and he who rejects you rejects me and the One who sent me' (Luke 10:16). We have come to know the dispensation of our salvation through none other than those through whom the Gospel came to us. First of all, they preached the Gospel; then, by the will of God, they transmitted it to us in the Scriptures to be the foundation and pillar of our faith . . . After our Lord had risen from the dead, and after the Holy Spirit had come upon them, investing them with power from on high (cf Luke 24:49), they were filled with all His gifts and possessed perfect knowledge *(gnosis)*. They went to the ends of the earth, proclaiming the good news of the good things which come from God, and announcing heavenly peace to men. All of them together and each of them on his own possesed the Gospel of God . . . They have all passed on to us this teaching: that there is one God, the Creator of heaven and earth, who was announced by the Law and the prophets, and one Christ, the Son of God. Anyone who refuses to assent to these truths shows contempt for the 'partakers of the Lord' (cf Heb. 3:14), indeed for the Lord Himself and for the Father; such a person condemns himself, because he resists and opposes his salvation — that is what all the heretics do.

When Scripture is used to demolish their arguments, [the heretics] turn round and start accusing Scripture itself: they say that it is inaccurate and untrustworthy, that its language is ambiguous, and that the truth cannot be extracted from it by people ignorant of their [secret] tradition . . . Each of them claims that this wisdom is his own discovery . . . but they are all so thoroughly perverted that they deprave the rule of truth and shamelessly preach themselves.

But when we appeal to the tradition that comes from the apostles, the tradition preserved in the Churches thanks to the succession of presbyters, they oppose tradition. They claim to be wiser than not only the presbyters but the apostles themselves, and to have discovered the pure truth.

They allege that the apostles mixed the prescriptions of the Law with the words of the Saviour. Indeed, they say that not only the apostles but the Lord Himself uttered words which came from 'Demiurge' or the 'Intermediary' . . .

These, my dear friend, are our adversaries. Like slippery snakes, they try to escape at every point. They must, therefore, be opposed at every point in the hope that, by our refutation, at least some of them may be converted to the truth.   III 1, 1–2, 3

(145) The tradition of the apostles, which has been manifested throughout the world, can be examined by all who want to see the truth. We can enumerate the bishops instituted by the apostles in the Churches, and their successors down to our own day. These men neither taught nor knew of anything like what [the heretics] rave about. Had the apostles known of abstruse mysteries to be taught to the 'perfect' and kept from everyone else, they would have passed them on especially to those to whom they entrusted the Churches. For they wanted their successors, the ones to whom they bequeathed their teaching office, to be blameless in all things (cf 1 Tim. 3:2). If these men carried out their mission correctly, it would be a great boon, but if they failed, an appalling calamity.

It would be too tedious, in a work like this, to go through the succession lists of all the Churches. We shall, therefore, take just one, the greatest, most ancient Church, the Church known to all, the Church founded and established in Rome by the two most glorious apostles, Peter and Paul. By showing that the tradition which she received from the apostles, the faith which she proclaims to men, has come down to us through the succession of bishops, we confute all those who, in whatever manner, . . . set up conventicles. With this Church, because of its more excellent origin, every Church (in other words, the faithful everywhere) must agree.

[*Now follows a proof of the uninterrupted succession of the twelve bishops from Peter to Eleutherus. The third of these is the author of the important Epistle of Clement.*] This is a most complete proof of the unity and identity of the life-giving faith, which has been preserved in the Church from the apostles until now and handed down in truth. III 3, 1—3

(146) With such proofs as these, we do not need to seek the truth elsewhere; it is easy to obtain it from the Church. In the most thorough way, the apostles have amassed in the Church, as in a treasure chest, all that pertains to the truth, so that everyone who so desires may drink the water of life (cf Apoc. 22:17). She is the entrance to life; all the others are thieves and robbers (cf John 10:8). We must, therefore, reject them, but love with the greatest zeal everything to do with the Church and lay hold of the tradition of truth. What does this come down to? Well, if controversy arises about some minor matter, should we not have recourse to the most ancient Churches, the one which had contact with the apostles, in order to obtain a sure and accurate resolution of the disputed issue? And supposing the apostles had not left us their writings, would we not then have to follow the order of the tradition which they handed down to the men to whom they entrusted the Churches?

Many of the barbarian nations who believe in Christ have given their assent to this order. Salvation has been written in their hearts (2 Cor. 3:3), without paper and ink, by the Spirit. Preserving the ancient tradition, they believe in one God, the Creator of heaven and earth and everything in them, and in Christ Jesus our Lord, who, in His superabundant love for His creation, condescended to be born of the Virgin, uniting man to God through Himself, who suffered under Pontius Pilate, rose again and was taken up in splendour, who will come in glory as Saviour of those who are saved . . . Thanks to the ancient tradition of the apostles, they reject, even in thought, the lying inventions [of the heretics]. III 4, 1—2

(147) Since the tradition which comes down from the apostles exists in this way in the Church and abides among us, let us return to the scriptural proof provided by those of the apostles who wrote the gospels. In their writings they expounded the doctrine of God, showing that our Lord Jesus Christ is the truth (cf John 14:6), and that no lie is in him (cf 1 Peter 2:22; 1 John 2:21,27) . . . The apostles, being disciples of the Truth, are above all falsehood. Falsehood has no partnership with the truth, just as light has nothing in common with darkness (cf 2 Cor. 6:14); the presence of the one excludes the other. Our Lord, being the Truth, did not tell lies. If He had known of some being that was the 'fruit of a fall', He would never have acknowledged Him as God, the Lord of all, King Most High, and His own Father.

The Lord implanted [true] knowledge in His disciples. Through it He cured the sick and turned sinners from their sin. He did not conform His speech to their earlier [Old Testament] opinions, nor His answers to the prejudices of His questioners. No, He spoke in accordance with the doctrine of salvation, without hypocrisy or respect of person.   III 5, 1—2

(148) Anyone who reads the Scriptures in this way will find in them a message about Christ and a foreshadowing of the new vocation [i.e., the new covenant]. He is the 'treasure hidden in the field' (cf Matt. 13:44) . . . hidden in the Scriptures. For He was pointed out by types and parables, which, humanly speaking, could not be understood before the prophecies were fulfilled, that is to say, before the coming of Christ. That is why the prophet Daniel was told: 'Shut up the words, and seal the book, until the time of the fulfilment, until many learn, and knowledge be complete. At that time, when the dispersion comes to an end, they will know all these things' (cf Dan. 12:4,7) . . . For this reason, when the Law is read by the Jews in our own time, it is like a fable, because they lack the explanation of everything relating to the Son of God's coming as man. But

when it is read by Christians, it really is the 'treasure hidden in the field', made clear and explained by the Cross of Christ . . . This was how the Lord expounded it for His disciples after His resurrection from the dead. He showed them, from Scripture itself, that 'it was necessary for the Christ to suffer and enter into His glory' (cf Luke 24:26), and that 'the remission of sins should be preached in His name throughout the world' (cf Luke 24:47) . . .

We must, therefore, obey the presbyters in the Church. They are the successors of the apostles, and by the Father's good pleasure, they have received, together with the succession in the episcopate, the sure charism of the truth.

The others, the people who have broken away from the original succession to set up in various places conventicles of their own, are to be regarded with suspicion. They are heretics with false opinions, or schismatics puffed up and self-indulgent, or again hypocrites interested only in money and vainglory . . . There are some who are regarded by many as presbyters. In fact, they serve their own lusts and do not give the fear of God priority in their hearts. They insult other people and swell with pride at the thought of their superior position . . . Of them the Lord said: 'If the wicked servant says to himself, "My master is delayed", and begins to beat his fellow servants and maids, and eats and drinks and gets drunk, the master of that servant will come on a day he is not expecting and at an hour he does not know, and will cut him short and assign him a place with the unbelievers' (Matt. 24:48ff).

We must keep away from all such persons, but stay close to those who, as we have said, preserve the succession of the apostles, and who, together with the order of priesthood, display sound speech and blameless conduct as an example to others and for their improvement . . . As St Paul, with a good conscience, said to the Corinthians: 'We are not, like so many, adulterators of God's Word, but with sincerity, as from God, before God in Christ we speak' (2 Cor. 2:17) . . . Such priests nourish the Church . . . St Paul tells us where we can find them: 'God has appointed in the Church first apostles, second prophets, third teachers' (1 Cor. 12:28). Where God has placed His gifts, we must learn the truth, that is to say, from those in whom we find succession from the apostles in the Church, sound and blameless conduct, and incorruptible purity of teaching.

IV 26, 1—5

Jews and Gentiles

(149) It is the 'one God' who led the patriarchs towards His dispensations, and 'justified the circumcised by faith and the uncircumcised through faith' (cf Rom. 3:30). Just as we [the Gentiles] were prefigured and heralded in the first, so they [the Jews] find their completed form in us, that is to say, in the Church, and there they receive the reward for their labours. As the Lord said to His disciples . . . 'In this is the saying true: one sows, another reaps' (John 4:37). It is clear that the patriarchs and prophets . . . foreshadowed our faith and sowed the coming of the Son of God on earth . . . This is why Philip, on finding the eunuch of the Queen of Ethiopia reading the words of Isaiah, 'He was led as a sheep to the slaughter . . .' (cf Acts 8:32f; cf Is. 53:7), and all the other details of [the Lord's] Passion and coming in the flesh, easily convinced the eunuch to believe that Jesus Christ, who was crucified under Pontius Pilate and suffered everything foretold by the prophet, really is the Son of God who gives eternal life to men. As soon as he had baptized him, Philip left the eunuch. He had already been instructed by the prophets, so there was nothing he lacked. He was ignorant not of God the Father, nor of the rules of moral life, but only of the coming of the Son of God . . .

The Fathers heralded things in a fatherly way, the prophets prefigured things in a legal way, [Christians], endowed with the grace of adoption, give to things a form corresponding to their conformity to Christ, and all things are shown forth by one God. Abraham was only one man, but he prefigured in his own person the two covenants, in which some sowed while others reaped . . . The patriarchs and prophets sowed the word about Christ, but the Church reaped it, that is, received the fruit.   IV 22, 2—25, 3

(150) [Through Isaiah] the Lord Himself has given us a sign, in the depth below and in the height above (cf Is. 7:11ff). Mankind [in the person of King Ahaz] did not ask for it, because he never expected that a Virgin, while remaining a virgin, could conceive and give birth to a Son. Mankind never expected that this Son would be 'God with us' (cf Is. 7:14), that He would descend into the lower parts of the earth (cf Eph. 4:9), seeking the lost sheep (cf Luke 15:4ff), in other words, His own handiwork. Mankind never expected that the Son would ascend to the height above, offering and commending to His Father the humanity He had found again, becoming in Himself the first fruits of humanity's resurrection, and that, as the Head had risen from the dead, so the rest of the Body (in other words, every man 'found' in Him who is Life (cf Phil. 3:9) would in turn rise again, once the time of punishment, due to disobedience, had been fulfilled; yes, that the Body, knit together and strengthened 'through its joints and liga- ments', would grow with the increase that comes from God (cf Col. 2:19), each member having its own proper and fit position in the Body. For there are many mansions in the Father's house (cf John 14:2), because there are many members in the Body (cf Rom. 12:4).   III 19, 3

(151) If someone believes in the one God, who made all things by the Word (as Moses says, 'And God said, "Let there be light", and there was light' (Gen. 1:3)), . . . he will, in the first place, be attached to the Head, 'from whom the whole Body is compacted and fitly joined together, and through every joint with which it is supplied, when each part is working properly, makes bodily growth and builds itself up in love' (Eph. 4:16). Then every word emanating from him will be trustworthy, provided he diligently reads

the Scriptures with the presbyters in the Church, for they, as we have shown, have the teaching of the apostles.

Now the apostles all taught that there are two Testaments for two peoples, but that it was one and the same God who decreed them both for the benefit of the human beings who, when the Testaments were given, would believe in God . . . We have already shown that the first Testament was not given in vain, without reason or by chance. First, it subdued its recipients for the service of God; this was for their own advantage, for God does need to be served by man. Secondly, it provided a type of heavenly things, because man could not yet see the things of God with his own eyes. It offered an anticipated image of the realities of the Church, in order to strengthen our faith, and it contained a prophecy of things to come to teach man that God has foreknowledge of all things.

(152) The truly 'spiritual' disciple is the one who has received the Spirit of God, the Spirit who, from the beginning, in all the dispensations of God, has been present to men, who announced things future, revealed things present, and explained things past. Such a disciple 'judges all men, but is himself judged by no man' (1 Cor. 2:15).

He judges the Gentiles, because they 'serve the creature rather than the Creator' (Rom. 1:25), and with a depraved mind waste their energy on vanity.

He also judges the Jews because they do not accept the Word of freedom, because they do not want to go off in liberty, even though the Liberator Himself was in their midst . . . They did not want to see that all the prophets proclaimed His two comings: at the first, He was a man covered in wounds, bearing our weakness (cf Is. 53:3) . . . at the second, He will come on the clouds [as judge] . . .

He also judges the doctrine of Marcion. How can there be two gods, separated from each other by an infinite distance? How can he be good who draws men who are not his own possession from their creator and invites them into his own kingdom? Why does his goodness fall short of saving all men? . . . And if the Lord came from a different Father, how could He say that the bread which is part of the creation to which we belong was His Body and affirm that the mixed cup was His Blood? . . . And if He was not flesh, but only seemed to be man, how could He have been crucified, and how could blood and water have streamed from His pierced side? . . .

And He judges all the disciples of Valentinus. With their lips they confess one God the Father, from whom all things come, but they also maintain that the Maker of all things is Himself the fruit of a fall. Similarly, with their lips they confess that there is one Lord Jesus Christ, the Son of God, but in their minds they think of the Only-begotten as one emission, the Word as another, Christ as another, and the Saviour as yet another. On their view, though these are spoken of as if they were one person, they are to be thought of as having a separate existence, each with his own emission according to the rank of his 'syzygy'. In other words, their lips assent to the unity, but their thoughts and minds, in 'searching the depths' (cf 1 Cor. 2:10), dissent to the unity, and so they come under the manifold judgement of God . . . Their own prophet Homer, under whose instruction they invented their doctrines, will, in fact, accuse them: 'Who dares think one thing, and another tell, my heart detests him as the Gates of Hell' (*Iliad* 9, 312–313, Alexander Pope's version). . .

He will judge the Ebionites, too . . . How can men leave behind birth into mortality without a new birth, a birth wonderfully and unexpectedly given by God as a sign of salvation? I mean the Virgin Birth [of the Son of God], which leads to the rebirth of men through faith . . . How could [Jesus] have been greater than Solomon and Jonah (cf Matt. 12:41f) and the Lord of David (cf Matt. 22:43), who was of the same substance as they were ? How could He have defeated him who was strong against man (cf Matt.

12:29), who had not only overcome man, but also held him in his power? How could He conquer the conqueror and liberate the conquered if He were not Himself greater than conquered man? Who else is superior to man, made in the image of God, who more excellent than the Son of God, to whose image man was made? . . .

He will also judge those who introduce [the idea that Christ was man only in] appearance. How can they imagine they are presenting a real argument when their Master is only an imaginary being? . . . How can they truly be partakers of salvation if the One they claim to believe manifested Himself only in appearance? . . .

He will also judge the false prophets, who have not received the prophetic charism from God, and do not fear God . . . He will also judge the instigators of schism, who are devoid of the love of God, more concerned with their own advantage than with the unity of the Church. For trivial reasons, for any reason that occurs to them, they tear up and divide the great and glorious Body of Christ. In fact, they do all they can to destroy it, speaking peace and making war . . . No reform could come from them that would be sufficient to make up for the harm caused by their schism.

Finally, he judges all those outside the truth, that is to say, outside the Church.   IV 32, 1—33, 1—7

The world at the service of believers

(153) God is, therefore, one and the same. He rolls up the heavens like a scroll (cf Is. 34:4) and renews the face of the earth (cf Ps. 103:30). He made things temporal for the sake of man, so that man, growing up up among them, might bear the fruit of immortality. And in His loving kindness, He clothes man with things eternal.   IV 5, 1

God's creation in the service of His redemption

(154) The Lord did not carry out His great plan of salvation by means of someone else's creation, but by His very own; not through things made out of 'ignorance' and 'defeat', but through things which owe their substance to the wisdom and power of the Father. He was neither unjust, coveting someone else's property, nor needy, incapable of bestowing life on His own through His own. No, He used His own creation for the salvation of man. Creation could never have borne Him if it had been an emission of 'ignorance' and 'defeat' . . . And even if it had been made by the angels . . . how could angelic handiwork have borne simultaneously the Father and the Son?   V 18, 1

The world serves believers

(155) Where do the houses we live in come from, and the clothes we wear, and the pots and pans we use, and everything else serving our daily life, if not from the things which, when we were pagans, we acquired through avarice, or from parents, relations, or friends, who obtained them unjustly, not to mention what we still acquire now we are in the faith? Who sells without wanting to get some money from the buyer? Who buys without wanting good value from the seller? Is there a businessman not in business to make a living? And those believers who are in the royal palace, do they not receive their income from the coffers of Caesar? And does not each of them, according to his ability, give to those in need? The Egyptians [who were plundered by the Jews] were indebted to the people not just for their material property but for their very lives, because of the kindness of the patriarch Joseph in former times. In what way are the heathen in debt to us, the heathen from whom we receive profit and advantage? What they produce by labour, we in the faith use without labour.   IV 30, 1

The Eucharist

The Eucharist is based on creation

(156) True, the Lord could have provided the wedding guests with wine and filled the hungry with food without using any pre-existing created thing. But that is not what He did. He took loaves which earth had given and gave thanks (cf John 6:11). It was the same when He changed the water into wine, satisfying those reclining at table and quenching the thirst of those invited to the wedding (cf Matt. 11:2—10); Apoc. 19:9). By so doing, He showed that the God who made the earth and commanded it to bear fruit (cf Gen. 1:11), who establishd the waters and brought forth the fountains (cf Gen. 1:9), has in these last times granted mankind, through His Son, the blessing of food and the grace of drink, the Incomprehensible through the Comprehensible, the Invisible through the Visible [the incarnate Son].   III 11, 5

(157) They are totally foolish, these people who despise the whole saving plan of God, who deny the salvation of the flesh, and scorn its regeneration, claiming it is not capable of incorruptibility. If the flesh is not saved, the Lord did not redeem us by His Blood, the cup of the Eucharist is not communion in His Blood, and the bread we break is not communion in His Body. For blood can only come from veins, flesh, and whatever else makes up the substance of man. All this the Word of God really and truly became, in order to redeem us by His Blood. As the apostle says, 'In Him we have redemption through His Blood, the remission of sins' (Col. 1:14).

And because we are His members, we are nourished by means of creation, the creation which He Himself gives us by making His sun to rise and sending the rain as He pleases (cf Matt. 5:45). The cup, which is part of creation, He declares to be His Blood, by which our own blood is fortified, and the bread, which is part of creation, He affirms to be His Body, by which our own body is fortified.

So then, if the mixed cup and the manufactured bread receive the Word of God and become the Eucharist, that is to say, the Blood and Body of Christ, which fortify and build up the substance of our flesh, how can these people claim that the flesh is incapable of receiving God's gift of eternal life, when it is nourished by Christ's Blood and Body and is His member? As the blessed apostle says in his letter to the Ephesians, 'For we are members of His Body, of His flesh and of His bones' (Eph. 5:30). He is not talking about some kind of 'spiritual' and 'invisible' man, 'for a spirit does not have flesh and bones' (Luke 24:39). No, he is talking of the organism possessed by a real human being, composed of flesh and nerves and bones. It is this which is nourished by the cup which is His Blood, and is fortified by the bread which is His Body. The stem of the vine takes root in the earth and eventually bears fruit, and 'the grain of wheat falls into the earth' (John 12:24), dissolves, rises again, multiplied by the all-containing Spirit of God, and finally, after skilled processing, is put to human use. These two then receive the Word of God and become the Eucharist, which is the Body and Blood of Christ. Similarly, our bodies, having been nourished by the Eucharist, having been laid to rest in the earth, and having there dissolved, will rise again at their appointed time, for the Word of God will grant them resurrection 'to the glory of God the Father' (cf Phil 2:11). He will clothe the mortal with immortality and freely bestow incorruptibility on the corruptible (cf 1 Cor. 15:53), for God's power is made perfect in weakness (cf 2 Cor. 12:9). So we must never become puffed up, as if we had the source of life within ourselves, asserting ourselves, with ungrateful minds, against God. In fact, experience should teach us that it is through God's grandeur and not our own nature that we possess eternal duration.   V 2, 2—3

The Eucharistic Sacrifice presupposes the Trinity

(158) It is right that we should make an oblation to God, and in all things show our gratitude to God our Maker, with a pure intention and a faith free of hypocrisy, in firm hope and fervent love, offering the first-fruits of His creation.

Only the Church offers the Creator this pure oblation, offering Him, with thanksgiving, things that are part of His creation. The Jews no longer offer, for their hands are full of blood; they did not accept the Word through whom an offering can be made to God. Nor do any of the conventicles of the heretics make an offering. For some of them say that the Father is different from the Creator, and so, in offering Him things from this created world of ours, they make Him look envious and covetous of someone else's property. Other heretics say that our world is the outcome of defect, ignorance, and passion, and so, when they offer Him the fruits of 'ignorance', 'passion', and 'defect', they sin against their Father, insulting Him rather than giving Him thanks. And how can they say that the bread over which thanks has been given is the Lord's Body and the cup His Blood, when they will not admit that that same Lord is the Son of the world's Creator, that is, His Word, through whom trees bear fruit, the fountains gush forth, and 'the earth gives first the blade, then the ear, then the full grain in the ear' (Mark 4:28)?

Then again, how can they say that the flesh, which is nourished with the Body and Blood of the Lord, falls into corruption and does not partake of life? They should either change their opinions or stop offering what we have just mentioned! Our opinion, however, is in harmony with the Eucharist, and the Eucharist confirms our opinion. For we offer Him His own, consistently proclaiming the communion and unity of flesh and Spirit. For just as the bread which comes from the earth, having received the invocation of God, is no longer ordinary bread, but the Eucharist, consisting of two realities, earthly and heavenly, so our bodies, having received the Eucharist, are no longer corruptible, because they have the hope of the resurrection. IV 18, 4—5

1 *Caput, kephalaion,* 'head' in the sense of 'seat', 'place of origin'.
2 On this passage, see the commentary in *Sources Chrétiennes 152,* pp. 286—295.
3 Certain sects celebrated the Eucharist only with water. Irenaeus sees in the mixing of water and wine in the Eucharist the symbol of the unity of the first and second creation, of nature and grace, of creature and Creator, in and through Christ.
4 The phrases in square brackets have been taken from the commentary in *Sources Chrétiennes 210* (p. 345) in order to clarify the meaning of this difficult passage. [Translator's note].
5 *Compendii poculo:* the Passion, through which He was to accomplish both the 'recapitulation' of salvation history and the final, wondrous 'mingling' of water (humanity) and wine (divinity). This is represented in the Eucharist and foreshadowed in the miracle at Cana.

Fulfilment in God

'Recapitulation' describes God's objective plan of salvation: the maturing of the earthly world in the strength of a grace that descends from above. Now comes the question of man's subjective fulfilment within this order of salvation. The Gnostics taught that human beings fall into two groups, the higher 'spiritual' and the lower 'carnal' or 'animal', of which only the former can partake of true and complete redemption. Consistently with this, they also taught that the material and bodily elements in the spiritual man are just an inessential shell, which is incapable of entering into the pure spirit's final state of perfection.

Irenaeus sees this as utterly anti-Christian. For him, the unity of body and soul is fundamental to the objective plan of salvation as revealed from above: as involving the unity of matter and spirit, law and love, nature and grace. So Gnostic 'spirituality' is replaced by the resurrection of the flesh as the ultimate affirmation of the complete and unabridged earthly world, the world of body as well as soul.

The indissoluble unity of body and soul is the sign that man is not a 'pure' anything. He is a creature, and so, in his innermost being, he is ordered, beyond himself, towards a Creator. This is expressed by the doctrine that man is made up essentially of three parts: body, soul, and spirit (pneuma). Spirit is the thing in man that is essentially more than man, something which does not 'rise from below' but 'comes down from above'. Like all the Fathers, Irenaeus is thinking of just the concrete (supernatural) order of the world; the call to grace and the life of grace belong to the concrete integrity of man. The doctrine of these three elements in man ('trichotomism') is, therefore, to be regarded as a first attempt, admittedly not a fully worked-out one, at understanding the relationship of nature and grace.

The same is true of the view, also held by other writers of the period, that the soul is only 'imperishable' by grace. Imperishability (aphtharsia) here means both natural im-

mortality and engraced eternal glory; the two aspects have not yet been separated.

The background to this doctrine is a vivid idea of man's profound dependence on, and adherence to, God. He does not so much 'exist' as 'partake'. This leads to the idea of the creature's eternal becoming: even in heaven, in the vision of God face-to-face, there is a further, eternal movement into the ever new depths of the ever greater God.

Soul between body and spirit

(159) Just as the animated body is not itself the soul, but partakes of the soul as long as God wills, so the soul is not life, but partakes of the life God gives it. That is why the prophetic word says of the first man: 'He was made a living soul' (Gen. 2:7). This teaches us that it is by participation in life that the soul is made alive; in other words, the soul and the life that is in it are to be seen as two separate things. Thus, when God gives life and perpetual duration, souls which had no previous existence begin from that moment to have permanent existence; it is, after all, God who wills them both to be and to continue to be. For God's will must govern and hold sway in all things. Everything else must yield to Him, be submitted to Him, be devoted to His service.   II 34, 4

(160) The soul and the spirit (*pneuma*) may be part of man, but they are certainly not the man. The complete man is a mixture and a union: the soul, which has received the Spirit of the Father, mixed with the flesh fashioned in the image of God . . .

If you take away the substance of the flesh, in other words, the shaped clay, and consider just the naked spirit, what you are left with is not 'the spiritual man', but merely 'the spirit of a man' or 'the Spirit of God'. However, when this Spirit is blended with the soul and united to the shaped clay, the result, thanks to the outpouring of the Spirit, is a spiritual and complete man, and it is this, the complete man, who is made in the image and likeness of God.

When the Spirit is missing from the soul, you have a being which, though truly animal and carnal, is incomplete. It may have the 'image' in the shaped clay, but it lacks the 'likeness' given by the Spirit. Such a being is incomplete, and so too is what results from taking away the image and rejecting the shaped clay. It can no longer be thought of as a man, but as either part of a man or something other than a man. The shaped clay of the flesh is not, on its own, a complete man, but just the body of a man, a part of a man. Similarly, the soul, on its own, is not a man, but just the soul of a man, a part of a man. And the Spirit is not a man: Spirit is called 'Spirit', not 'man'. It is, then, the mixture and union of all these things which makes the complete man. Thus the apostle, in his first letter to the Thessalonians, explains that the redeemed man is the complete and spiritual man: 'May the God of peace sanctify you completely, and may your whole being, spirit and soul and body, be kept blameless at the coming of the Lord Jesus Christ' (1 Thess. 5:23).   V 6, 1

(161) As we have shown, the complete man is made up of these three things — flesh, soul, and Spirit. One of these saves and forms, namely, the Spirit; another is saved and formed, namely, the flesh; another finds itself between the other two, namely, the soul. Sometimes the soul follows the Spirit, and then, with the Spirit's help, it takes flight. Sometimes it gives in to the flesh, and then it falls into earthly lusts.   V 9, 1

The soul's free decision
(162) John the Baptist . . . says of Christ: 'He will baptize you with the Holy Spirit and with fire. His winnowing fork is in His hand to clear His threshing-floor, and to gather the wheat into his granary, but the chaff he will burn with

unquenchable fire' (Luke 3:16f). He who makes the wheat and He who makes the chaff are not two different persons, but one and the same: it is He who judges them, that is to say, separates them. Now, of course, wheat and chaff are things which by nature lack soul and reason; this is the way they have been made. But man is rational, and in that respect he is like God. He has been created with free will and self-determination; he himself is the cause of his becoming sometimes wheat, sometimes chaff. He will, therefore, justly be judged, because, having been made rational, he has lost true rationality; by living irrationally, he has worked against the justice of God, giving himself up to every earthly spirit and serving every lust. As the prophet says, 'Man, for all his dignity, did not understand; match him with the brute beasts, and he is no better than they' (Ps. 48:21; Knox translation adapted).   IV 4, 3

(163) Since all good things are with God, those who by their own choice fly from God defraud themselves of all good things. Consequently, defrauded of all the good things that are with God, they fall under the just judgement of God.   IV 39, 4

(164) [The wicked] do not receive the Word of incorruption, but remain in mortal flesh. They are the debtors of death, because they do not accept the antidote of life.   III 19, 1

(165) Those who do not have the element that saves, that forms and vivifies, will be, and are called, 'flesh and blood', because they do not have the Spirit of God within them. That is why the Lord calls them 'dead' (cf Luke 9:60). V 9, 1

'Psychic' breath and 'pneumatic' spirit
(166) The 'breath of life' (cf Gen. 2:7), which makes man an animated ['psychic'] being, is not the same as the 'life-giving Spirit' (cf 1 Cor. 15:45), which makes him spiritual.

That is why Isaiah says: 'Thus says the Lord, who made the heavens and established them, who founded the earth and things it contains, who gives breath to the people upon it and the spirit to those who tread upon it' (Is. 42:5). What he is saying is that the 'breath' is given to all the people on earth without exception, whereas the Spirit is given exclusively to those who 'tread' down all earthly lusts. Isaiah makes the same distinction when he says: 'From me proceeds the Spirit, and I have made the breath of life' (Is. 57:16). He puts 'the Spirit' in His proper place within the Godhead: this is the Spirit whom God, in these last times, has poured out on the human race to give us adoption as His sons. By contrast, he situates the 'breath of life' within the general order of creation, showing it to be something created. Now there is a difference between what is made and the one who makes it. The breath is temporal, the Spirit eternal. The breath briefly increases in strength, continues for a certain time, and then departs, leaving its former abode breathless. But the Spirit, having pervaded man within and without, remains for ever and never leaves him.

'But', says the apostle, addressing us human beings, 'it is not the spiritual which is first but the psychic, and then spiritual' (1 Cor. 15:46). He has good reason for saying this. First, man had to be shaped; having been shaped, he had to be given a soul; then and only then did he receive the communion of the Spirit. The first Adam, therefore, 'was made a living soul, the second a life-giving spirit' (1 Cor. 15:45). He who was made a living soul turned to evil and lost life, but that very same man, when he returns to the good and receives the life-giving Spirit, shall find life.

V 12, 2

(167) The Lord also made it clear that, in addition to being called, we ought to be adorned with the works of justice, so that the Spirit of God might rest upon us. This is the wedding garment of which the apostle says: 'Not that we would be unclothed, but that we would be further clothed,

so that what is mortal may be swallowed up by life' (2 Cor. 5:4).   IV 36, 6

(168) Man is in as much need of communion with God as God is in need of nothing. For this is the glory of man: to persevere and remain in the service of God.   IV 14, 1

(169) How could they be saved unless it were God who effected their salvation on earth? How shall man go to God if God has not come to man?   IV 33, 4

The Gnostic doctrine of fulfilment

(170) When all the [spiritual] seed [in the world] comes to perfection, they say that their Mother, Achamoth [the sensible manifestation of divine Wisdom], leaves her place at the centre of the world and enters the 'Pleroma', and there she welcomes her Saviour, who was formed out of all [thirty Aeons], to bring about the 'syzygy' of the Redeemer and 'Wisdom' or Achamoth [they are merged into a single androgynous being]. These, then, are the 'Bridegroom and Bride', while the bridal chamber is the full extent of the Pleroma. The 'spiritual', having cast off their souls and become again pure intellectual spirits, enter the Pleroma, unhindered and unseen, so as to be given as brides to the angels who accompany the Saviour. As for the Demiurge, he takes over the place of his mother, 'Wisdom', at the centre of the world. The souls of the just are supposed to rest in this central place, because nothing 'psychic' can go into the Pleroma. When all this has been accomplished, the fire hidden in the world will blaze up, catch hold of the entire material world, and consume it. At the same time it will itself be extinguished and disappear into nothingness.
                                                                                        I 7, 1

First Objection

(171) Man's intellect, thought,[1] mental intention, and so on are not realities existing independently of the soul. They are movements and operations of the soul itself, with no existence outside the soul. What part of them, then, will be left over to enter into the Pleroma? Inasmuch as they are souls, they remain in the central place; inasmuch as they are bodies, they burn along with the rest of matter.

II 29, 3

Second Objection

(172) It is obvious that acts of justice are performed in bodies.[2] One of two things follows from this: either all souls go off by necessity to the centre of the world, and there will never be a judgement [and no moral recompense]; or the bodies which have partaken of justice reach the place of refreshment together with the souls which have likewise partaken. This will happen only if justice is powerful enough to transport to that place those which have partaken of it. Then the doctrine of the resurrection of the body will emerge true and certain. That is the faith which we hold. We believe that when God resurrects our mortal bodies, which have preserved justice, He will make them incorruptible and immortal. For God is superior to nature. He has within Him the will to do it, because He is good; the power to do it, because He is mighty; and He perfects it, because He Himself is rich and perfect.   II 29, 2

The possibility of resurrection

(173) They show contempt for the power of God . . . when they dwell on the weakness of the flesh and ignore the strength of Him who raises the flesh from the dead (cf Heb. 11:19). If God did not give life to the mortal and raise up the corruptible to incorruptibility (cf 1 Cor. 15:53), He would no longer be mighty. But to see that He is in all things mighty,

we need only to consider our own beginnings, since God took dust from the earth and formed man. It is surely much more difficult, incredibly difficult, to make an existing human being — indeed, an animated, rational human being — out of non-existent bones, nerves, and veins, in the absence, in fact, of everything that goes to make up the human organism. This, I say, is much more difficult than restoring already created man . . . once he has decomposed into the earth.   V 3, 2

(174) The flesh will be found capable of receiving and containing the power of God, since at the beginning it received the art of God, so that one part of it became the eye for seeing, another the ear for hearing, another the hand for touching and working . . . Consequently, the flesh is not excluded from the wisdom and power of God. His life-giving power is 'made perfect in weakness' (cf 2 Cor. 12:9), in other words, in the flesh. Now if, as these people say, the flesh is incapable of receiving the life which God gives, will they please either tell us that they are here and now alive and partaking of life, or admit that they have absolutely nothing to do with life and are at present dead! But if they are dead, how can they move and speak and do all the other things which the living, but not the dead, can do? And if they are here and now alive and partaking of life, how do they dare to say that the flesh does not partake of life? After all, they admit that *they* have life at present. It is like holding a sponge full of water or a blazing torch and claiming that sponges cannot hold water and torches cannot take fire . . . This temporal life is so much feebler than eternal life, and yet it is strong enough to give life to our mortal members. If so, why should eternal life, which is so much more powerful, not vivify the flesh, which is trained and accustomed to bear life?   V 3, 2—3

(175) By the very same Hands which fashioned them at the beginning, [Enoch and Elijah] were taken up and away. In

Adam, the Hands of God were accustomed to guide, hold, and carry Their handiwork, and to transport and place it wherever They pleased. Now where was the first man placed? In Paradise, of course ... From there, because of his disobedience, he was thrown out. And there, according to the presbyters who are disciples of the apostles, [these two] were transferred. For Paradise was prepared for men who are just and have the Spirit. It was there that St Paul, having been caught up, heard things which cannot be told (cf 2 Cor. 12:4). And there, too, as a prelude to incorruptibility, remain those who have been transported until the final consummation.

Now some people may think that it is impossible for human beings to remain alive for such a long time, that Elijah was not taken up in the flesh, and that his flesh was consumed in the chariot of fire. If they think like that, they ought to recall that Jonah, having been thrown into the depths of the sea and swallowed by the whale, was, by the command of God, vomited out safe and sound on dry land. Hananiah, Azariah, and Mishael were thrown into the seven-times heated fiery furnace, and yet suffered not the slightest harm; not even the smell of fire was on them. If the Hand of God was with them and achieved in them things so extraordinary and impossible for human nature, is it any wonder that [this same Hand], in carrying out the Father's will, should accomplish something extraordinary in those who have been transported? Now the 'Hand' I am speaking about is the Son of God. In the words Scripture ascribes to Nebuchadnezzar: 'Did we not throw three men into the furnace? But I see four men walking around in the midst of the fire, and the fourth is like the Son of God' (Dan. 3:19f). Therefore, neither the nature of any creature nor the infirmity of the flesh can be stronger than the will of God. God is not subject to created things; created things are subject to God, and all things serve His will.

V 5, 1—2

(176) As the Lord says, though 'the flesh is weak', 'the Spirit' is eager (cf Matt. 26:41), in other words, capable of doing whatever He is eager to do. If, then, you join the eagerness of the Spirit, as a kind of spur, to the weakness of the flesh, the strong inevitably prevails over the weak. The weakness of the flesh will be swallowed up by the strength of the Spirit, and because of the communion of Spirit [and flesh], such a person will no longer be carnal but spiritual . . . Once swallowed up, the weakness of the flesh reveals the power of the Spirit, and the Spirit, in absorbing its weakness, takes possession of the flesh as His own inheritance. It is from these two that the living man is made. He is living because of the participation of the Spirit; he is man because of the substance of the flesh.

Thus the flesh without the Spirit of God is dead, without life, incapable of inheriting the Kingdom of God. It is like blood, like water poured out on the ground. That is why the apostle says: 'As was the man of earth, so are those who are of earth' (cf 1 Cor. 15:48). But where the Spirit of the Father is, there is a living man. The rational blood is preserved by God for vengeance (cf Apoc. 6:10), and the flesh is possessed by the Spirit, forgets itself, puts on the qualities of the Spirit, and is conformed to the Word of God. As Scripture says, 'Just as we have borne the image of him who is of earth, so we shall bear the image of Him who is from heaven' (1 Cor. 15:49). What is earthly? The handiwork. What is heavenly? The Spirit . . .

Strictly speaking, the flesh does not inherit; it is inherited. As the Lord says, 'Blessed are the meek, for they shall inherit the earth' (Matt. 5:5), as if in the Kingdom the earth, from which the substance of our flesh comes, will be possessed as an inheritance. And so He wants the temple to be pure, so that God's Spirit might delight in it, as the bridegroom in his bride. Just as the bride does not take the bridegroom but is taken by him when he comes to make her his own, so the flesh, in itself and on its own, cannot inherit and take possession of the Kingdom of God, but it can be inherited and possessed by the Spirit in the Kingdom, for the living inherit the goods of the deceased. Now inheriting and being inherited are two different things. The inheritor rules and commands, and disposes of his inheritance as he wants to. The inheritance, by contrast, is subject to him, obeys him, is ruled by him, is under his control. Who, then, is the living? The Spirit of God. And what are the goods of the deceased? The various parts of man which rot in the earth. It is these which are inherited by the Spirit and transported into the Kingdom of Heaven.   V 9, 2—4

(177) At present we receive a part of His Spirit to perfect us and to prepare us for incorruptibility. In this way we become gradually accustomed to receiving and bearing God. The apostle calls this gift a 'pledge' (cf Eph. 1:14), in other words, a part of the honour promised us by God . . . This 'pledge' here and now dwells in us and makes us spiritual. The mortal is swallowed up by immortality (cf 2 Cor. 5:4), for 'you are not in the flesh, but in the Spirit, if the Spirit of God really dwells in you' (Rom. 8:9). What is more, this is achieved not by casting off the flesh, but by communion with the Spirit; after all, the people to whom St Paul was writing were not fleshless beings, but simply those who had received the Spirit of God, in whom we cry 'Abba, Father' (cf Rom. 8:15). Therefore, if, even now, we have the 'pledge' and cry 'Abba, Father', how wonderful it will be when we rise again and behold Him face to face, when all the members burst forth into a hymn of exultation, glorifying Him who raised them from the dead and gave them eternal life! If the simple pledge, wrapping itself round man, makes him cry 'Abba, Father', what will be achieved by the complete grace of the Spirit when it is given by God to men? It will make us like Him and accomplish the will of the Father, because it will make man after the image and likeness of God. Those, then, who have the pledge of the Spirit and are not enslaved to the lusts of the flesh, but submit themselves to the Spirit . . . are rightly

called 'spiritual' by the apostle (cf 1 Cor. 2:15; 3:1). Such spiritual persons are not bodiless spirits, but our very substance, that is, the union of soul and flesh, which, when it receives the Spirit of God, constitutes the spiritual person.   V 8, 1—2

(178) He says this lest, in pampering the flesh, we reject the grafting of the Spirit. For 'you, a wild olive tree, have been grafted into a cultivated olive tree and made a partaker of its sap' (cf Rom. 11:17,24). Now if a wild olive tree, after being grafted into a cultivated tree, remains what it was before, it is 'cut down and thrown into the fire' (cf Matt. 7:19). If, on the other hand, it accepts the grafting and is transformed into the cultivated olive tree, it becomes a fruit-bearing olive, planted, so to speak, in the garden (*paradiso*) of the king. The same is true of human beings. If, by faith, they make real progress towards the better, and receive God's Spirit and bring forth His fruits, they will be 'spiritual', planted, so to speak, in the garden (*paradiso*) of God. But if they reject the Spirit and remain what they were before, preferring to be of the flesh rather than of the Spirit, it is rightly said of them: 'Flesh and blood shall not inherit the Kingdom of God' (1 Cor. 15:50); in other words, the wild olive is not admitted into the garden of God.

In his parable of flesh and blood and the olive tree, the apostle has given us a wonderful description of our nature and of the whole saving plan of God. A cultivated olive, if neglected and left for a time to run to wood, begins to bear wild fruit, and becomes itself a wild olive. On the other hand, if the wild olive is carefully tended and grafted, it returns to the pristine fruitfulness of its nature. The same is true of human beings. If they are negligent, they bear the wild fruit of carnal lust, and by their own fault are unfruitful in justice. For it is while men sleep that the enemy sows the seeds of weeds (cf Matt. 13:25), which is why the Lord commands His disciples to keep watch (cf Matt. 24:42). On the other hand, those who have been unfruitful in justice and, so to speak, caught up in brambles can, if they are carefully tended and accept the grafting of the Word (cf James 1:21), return to the pristine nature of man, the nature, that is, which was created in the image and likeness of God. Just as grafted wild olive does not lose the substance of its wood, but changes the quality of its fruit . . . so man, when he is grafted in by faith and receives the Spirit of God, does not lose the substance of flesh, but changes the quality of those fruits which are his works.

V 10, 1–2

Eternal life is a grace

(179) The objection could at this point be made that souls which have only lately begun to exist cannot go on existing indefinitely. It could be argued that there are only two possibilities: either they must be without birth and beginning, if they are to be immortal, or they must die when the body dies, if they have had a beginning by birth.

To this we reply that only God, the Lord of all, is without beginning and end, remaining truly and for ever and unchangeably the same. As for the things which come from Him, whatever has been made, whatever is made, has a beginning of existence; they are inferior to their Maker precisely because they are not without beginning. They nevertheless continue and prolong their existence through the length of days in accordance with the will of God their Maker. He gives them first a beginning, then being.

The heavens above us — the firmament, sun, and moon, the stars in all their beauty — were created when previously they did not exist, and they continue indefinitely in accordance with God's will. Any right-thinking person will see that the same is true of souls, spirits, and every other created thing without exception. All creatures have a beginning of existence, but they continue to exist as long as God wills them to exist and to continue to exist. The prophetic Spirit bears witness to this doctrine when He says: 'He spoke, and they were made; He commanded, and they were created. He established them for ever, and for the ages of ages' (Ps. 148:5—6). Again, he says this of the salvation of man: 'He asked life of you, and you gave him length of days for the ages of ages' (Ps. 20:5). In other words, the Father of all grants continued existence 'for the ages of ages' to the redeemed. For life does not come from ourselves, nor from our nature, but is given by God as a grace. The person, therefore, who preserves the gift of life and gives thanks to the One who gave it to him will receive 'length of days for the ages of ages'. But the person who rejects that gift, who shows only ingratitude to his Creator for the gift of being created, and does not recognize the Giver, such a person deprives himself of continuance 'for the ages of ages'.[3]   II 34, 2—3

(180) To those who keep their love for God, He grants communion with Him. And communion with God is life and light and enjoyment of all the good things He has in store. But on those who, by their own choice, turn away from Him, He inflicts the separation which they themselves have chosen. And separation from God is death; separation from the light is darkness; separation from God is the loss of all the good things He has in store. Those, then, who by their apostasy have lost these things, who are destitute of all good, experience every kind of punishment. God does not punish them immediately of Himself; no, punishment comes upon precisely because they are destitute of all good . . . 'He who does not believe', says the Lord, 'is already judged' (John 3:18).   V 27, 2

(181) ['Man shall not live by bread alone, but by every word that proceeds from the mouth of God', Matt. 4:4; cf Deut. 8:3] By this commandment the Lord is teaching us, the redeemed. When we are hungry, He says, we should wait for the food given by God. If we are placed at the

summit of all grace, confident in our works of justice and adorned with excellent ministries, we must not swell with pride, nor tempt God, but should feel humility in all things and have this as our watchword: 'You shall not tempt the Lord your God' (Matt. 4:7; Deut. 6:16). The apostle's teaching was the same: 'Do not be haughty, but associate with the humble' (Rom. 12:16). We must not be carried away by wealth and worldly glory and passing fancy, but should know that we must worship 'the Lord your God' and serve Him alone (cf Matt. 4:10; Deut. 6:13). And we must not heed him who promises what is not his own: 'All these I will give you, if you will fall down and worship me' (Matt. 4:9). He himself admits that to worship him and to do his will is to fall from the glory of God. What sweet and good thing is there for such a fallen man to share? What can he hope for or expect except death? For the fallen man's nearest neighbour is death.   V 22, 2

Freedom as grace

(182) 'How often would I have gathered your children together as a hen gathers her brood under her wings, and you would not!' (Matt. 23:37). These words [of Christ] illustrate the ancient law of human freedom. For God made man free. From the beginning he has had his own power, just as he has had his own soul, to enable him, voluntarily and without coercion, to make God's mind his own. God does not use force, but good will is in Him always. He, therefore, gives good counsel to all things, but in men, as in the angels (angels, after all, are rational beings), He has placed the power of choice. The obedient were to possess, in all justice, the good which He had given and they had preserved, while the disobedient were, in all justice, to be found without the good and to receive the punishment they deserved . . . If, however, some had been made bad by nature and others good, the good would not deserve praise

for being good, because that was the way they were made, nor would the bad be blameworthy, because that was the way *they* were made.   IV 37, 1—2

(183) If all souls go to the place of refreshment on account of their nature and belong to the 'centre of the world' just because they are souls, then faith is superfluous, and the descent of the Saviour is superfluous. If, on the other hand, it is on account of their justice, then it is no longer because they are souls, but because they are just.   II 29, 1

(184) Just as God does not need what comes from us, so we do need to offer something to God. As Solomon says, 'He who has pity on the poor lends to God' (Prov. 19:17). For God, who needs nothing, accepts our good works so that He can give us in return His own things (cf Prov. 19:17). As Our Lord says, 'Come, you blessed of my Father, receive the Kingdom prepared for you. For I was hungry, and you gave me food. I was thirsty, and you gave me drink' (Matt. 25:34f) . . . He has no need of these things Himself, but He wants them to happen for our sake, so that we are not unfruitful. In the same way, the Word commanded the people to make offerings, though He did not need them, so that they would learn to serve God. It is, therefore, also His will that we should offer our gift at the altar frequently, indeed, without ceasing. For there is an altar in heaven; for it is to that place that our prayers and oblations are directed. And there is a temple: as St John says, 'the temple of God was opened' (Apoc. 11:9). And a tabernacle: 'Behold', he says, 'the tabernacle of God in which He dwelt with men' (Apoc. 21:3).   IV 18, 6

The eternal movement towards God

(185) Who are the pure? Those who steadily make their way by faith towards the Father and the Son.   V 8, 3

(186) To follow the Saviour is to partake of salvation, and to follow the light is to receive light.　　　　　　IV 14, 1

(187) [Abraham] rightly left all earthly kith and kin, and followed the Word of God. He wandered with the Word, so that He might abide with the Word. Rightly, too, did the apostles, of the race of Abraham, leave their ship and their father, and followed the Word of God. Rightly, too, do we, who have the same faith as Abraham, take up the Cross, as Isaac took up the wood (cf Gen. 22:6), and follow Him.
　　　　　　IV 5, 3—4

(188) It is right and fitting: God must always be ever greater, above all things . . . And not just in this world, but in the world to come as well, so that God might ever teach and man might ever learn the lessons taught by God. As the apostle says, when everything else has passed away, these three abide: faith, hope, and charity (cf 1 Cor. 13:9—13). Faith in our Master will remain ever firm, assuring us that there is only one true God, and that we should love Him for ever, for He alone is our Father, and that we should hope to receive and learn more and more from God, because He is good, and possesses boundless riches, a kingdom without end, and knowledge beyond measure.　　　　　　II 28, 3

(189) Those to whom God will say, 'Depart from me, you cursed, into the eternal fire' (Matt. 25:41), will be damned for ever. And those to whom He says, 'Come, you blessed of my Father, receive the Kingdom prepared for you for eternity' (Matt. 25:34), will receive the Kingdom and progress in it for ever.　　　　　　IV 28, 2

(190) Our face will see the face of God, and will be glad with an inexpressible joy, when, that is, it sees His joy.
　　　　　　V 7, 2

(191) If the revelation of God through creation bestows life on all who live on earth, how much more does the revelation of the Father through the Word bestow life on those who see God. IV 20, 7

(192) Just as those who see the light are in the light and share in its brightness, so those who see God are in God and receive His splendour. Now the splendour of God gives life; those who see God, therefore, receive life. That is why He who is uncontainable and incomprehensible and invisible presented Himself to be seen and comprehended and contained by men. He wanted to give life to those who receive and see Him. For just as His greatness is beyond measure, so His goodness is beyond expression. By that goodness, having been seen, he bestows life on those who see Him. It is impossible to live without life, and there is only life by participation in God. But to participate in God is to know God and to enjoy His goodness. Men will, therefore, see God that they may live, and by the vision they will be made immortal and attain God. IV 120, 5—6

1 The first objection to the Gnostics' spiritualistic doctrine of fulfilment has already been raised. It is a doctrine which rests upon an impossible isolation of the psychic/spiritual powers and activity from the substratum of the existing soul itself.

2 The second, even weightier objection emphasizes that, from the point of view of moral recompense, the soul together with the body, its instrument, demands eternal existence.

3 Irenaeus is not denying the continued existence of the wicked. But their souls are dead — and you do not say of dead bodies that they endure. Eternity, for him, signifies a supreme fulness. The sinful soul, by contrast, sinks into emptiness. Cf the following text.